Cuisines of Southeast Asia
THAI, VIETNAMESE, INDONESIAN, BURMESE & MORE

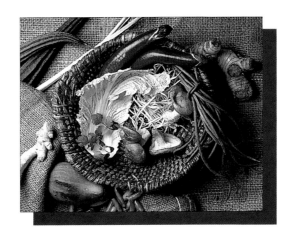

JAY HARLOW
Writer

SANDRA GARY
Editor

CALIFORNIA CULINARY ACADEMY

Jay Harlow, a freelance writer and cooking teacher, is author of several cookbooks and a weekly column in the *San Francisco Chronicle*. His other books for the California Culinary Academy cookbook series include *Enjoying American Wines; Chinese Cooking Techniques;* and *Classic American Cooking,* "The Pacific States" chapter. A former restaurant chef in California, he has also served on the board of directors of the San Francisco Professional Food Society, and was the first Administrative Director of the American Institute of Wine and Food.

The California Culinary Academy In the forefront of American institutions leading the culinary renaissance in this country, the California Culinary Academy in San Francisco has gained a reputation as one of the most outstanding professional chef training schools in the world. With a teaching staff recruited from the best restaurants of Western Europe, the Academy educates students from around the globe in the preparation of classical cuisine. The recipes in this book were created in consultation with the chefs of the Academy. For information about the Academy, write the Office of the Dean, California Culinary Academy, 625 Polk Street, San Francisco, CA 94102.

Front Cover
Chicken Saté, Sticky Rice Rolls and Chile-Fried Squid form the basis of a dinner buffet—the perfect way to introduce family and friends to Indonesian fare (page 96).

Title Page
A hand-made basket overflows with some of the fresh ingredients commonly used in Southeast Asian dishes (pages 23–31).

Back Cover

Upper Tender cubes of beef are simmered in a curry-like sauce, then skewered and grilled in Spiced Beef Saté (page 92).

Lower The curries of Burma reflect the influence of India, a close neighbor, as demonstrated by the flavors of Burmese Dry Pork Curry (page 78).

Special thanks to Ed Haverty, Helen Casartelli, Deborah Jones, Mustaffa Ismail, Sanuk San Francisco Fine Asian Collectibles

Contributors

Photographer
Ed Carey

Food Stylist
Sandra Cook

Photographic Stylist
Roz Baker

Calligraphers
Keith Carlson, Chuck Wertman

Illustrator
Frank Hildebrand

Additional Photographers
Laurie Black, Academy photography; Alan Copeland, at the Academy; Marshall Gordon, pages 17, 18, 19, 62, 71, 73, 101, 121; Kit Morris, author and chefs, at left; Kevin Sanchez, page 43; Jackson Vereen, page 55

Additional Photographic Stylist
Liz Ross, page 43

Additional Food Stylists
Doug Warne, pages 17, 18, 19, 62, 71, 73, 101, 121; Susan Massey-Weil, page 43; M. Susan Broussard, page 55

Copyeditor
Jessie Wood

Proofreader
Andrea Y. Connolly

Designers
Linda Hinrichs, Carol Kramer

Printed in Hong Kong through Mandarin Offset.

The California Culinary Academy series is published by the staff of Cole Group.

Publisher
Brete C. Harrison

VP and Director of Operations
Linda Hauck

VP Marketing and Business Development
John A. Morris

Associate Publisher
James Connolly

Director of Production
Steve Lux

Senior Editor
Annette Gooch

Production Assistant
Dotti Hydue

Address all inquiries to
Cole Group
4415 Sonoma Highway/ PO Box 4089
Santa Rosa, CA 95402-4089
(800) 959-2717 (707) 538-0492
FAX (707) 538-0497

Distributed to the book trade by Publishers Group West.

C O N T E N T S

*The mortar is a fitting symbol
of Southeast Asian cooking.
This tool is used every day to
combine the seasonings that are
the basic flavors of the region.*

The Cuisines of Southeast Asia

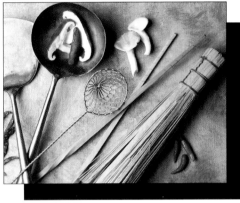

Fragrant curries; intricately spiced grilled meats; crisp, lightly cooked vegetables; subtly flavored soups, and fiery chile-flavored condiments—the cuisines of Southeast Asia offer such vibrant aromas, textures, and tastes as these. Yet the diverse dishes of Thailand, Burma, Laos, Cambodia, Vietnam, the Philippines, Malaysia, Indonesia, and Singapore are all based on a few cooking techniques that are easily mastered. This book helps you learn these basic techniques through authentic recipes and illustrated step-by-step procedures. The first chapter introduces the Asian style of eating, with a Special Feature on beverages that typically accompany meals (see page 20).

THE TASTES OF SOUTHEAST ASIA

Southeast Asia has always been a crossroads. Rich in natural resources and strategically located on the sea lanes that connect the Pacific and Indian oceans, the region has been visited repeatedly by traders and conquerors, each adding new ingredients and culinary influences to the local cuisines. Southeast Asian cooking includes such diverse elements as the fragrant spiced dishes of Indonesia and Malaysia; the clear-tasting simmered foods of Vietnam; the hybrid Chinese-Malay cooking of Singapore; the sometimes subtle, sometimes exuberant food of Thailand; and the Western-influenced cooking of the Philippines.

For all their diversity, there are common themes throughout the cuisines of Southeast Asia. The basic food resources of the region are similar. The widespread use of such ingredients as coconut milk, fresh coriander, and lemongrass gives unity to these cuisines, just as the various cuisines of southern Europe are related by their use of olive oil, tomatoes, and garlic, and the regional varieties of Chinese cooking, by the use of soy sauce, ginger, and green onion. Cooking techniques and dietary habits also cross national and ethnic boundaries.

Throughout this book are brief descriptions of the major cuisines of Southeast Asia, country by country. These notes give a glimpse of the cultural forces that helped shape each cuisine, as well as the favorite foods and flavor combinations that make each unique.

Rice is *the* staple food of Southeast Asia, nutritionally, economically, and symbolically. Whether eaten as cooked grains or ground into flour for noodles or other doughy foods, rice provides most of the calories in the everyday diet of most people. Like bread in the West, rice is a symbol of all food, and it has a prominent place in religious ritual.

Several other foods are used throughout the region. Coconut is perhaps the most important. At various stages of maturity the nut provides fresh juice, edible meat, and cooking oil; but most of it is used in the form of coconut milk, which moistens everything from curries to rice to desserts. Lemongrass gives a pleasant lemony aroma and flavor to savory dishes. Fresh and dried chiles, though not native to the region, are firmly established in every cuisine, alongside such native spices as cumin, coriander, and pepper. The various members of the ginger family, which includes the familiar ginger as well as turmeric and galangal, are important in every cuisine. Citrus trees grow throughout Southeast Asia, and cooks use their juice, peel, and leaves in cooking. The beanlike fruits of the tamarind tree provide another source of sour flavor. Various fermented and preserved fish and shellfish products, especially liquid fish sauce and fermented shrimp pastes, are also ubiquitous elements of Southeast Asian cuisine. All of these ingredients are discussed in the glossary beginning on page 24.

In addition to shared foodstuffs, the various cuisines of Southeast Asia rely on a similar set of cooking techniques. Although the details vary from one cuisine to the next, most Southeast Asian dishes are cooked by similar methods—simmering, stewing, steaming, frying, sautéing, or grilling. For this reason, recipes in this book are grouped into chapters according to cooking technique rather than by country of origin.

A WEALTH OF RESOURCES

Southeast Asia, as the term is used in this book, refers to the countries east of India and Bangladesh and south of China. For geographic and culinary purposes, the region can be divided into the mainland countries of Burma, Thailand, Laos, Cambodia, and Vietnam and the island countries of Indonesia, the Philippines, and Malaysia. Although the western, or peninsular, part of Malaysia is connected to the mainland, its characteristic foods are more like those of its island neighbors than those of the mainland.

Geographically this region is almost entirely tropical; only the northern-most part of Burma lies north of the Tropic of Cancer, and Indonesia straddles the equator. The major valleys of the mainland are drained by great rivers rising in the northern mountains—the Irrawaddy of Burma, the Chao Phraya of Thailand, the Red River of northern Vietnam, and the largest of all, the Mekong, which flows through or borders Laos, Thailand, Cambodia, and Vietnam before reaching the sea.

This is a region rich in agricultural resources. The fertile valleys of the mainland rivers are the rice bowls of Southeast Asia, producing abundant food both for the local population and for export. The islands, too, have fertile soil, mostly volcanic in origin, and are well watered by heavy rainfall. Rice farming in the islands is more difficult, but no less productive, thanks to abundant human energy. The rice terraces of Luzon in the Philippines, carved into the steep hillsides, are world famous. The island of Java contains some of the most intensively cultivated farmlands in the world, producing rice as well as all kinds of vegetables.

Throughout the region, coconut palms provide coconut meat, oil, and the ubiquitous coconut milk, not to mention thatching material, fibers, and fuel. Other trees bear a variety of tropical fruits—citrus, mango, papaya, and such local specialties as jackfruit and durian. Sugarcane vies for space with rice in some lowland areas. The highlands of Java, Sumatra, and other Indonesian islands produce some of the world's most famous coffees. The higher altitudes of the mainland produce fine teas and bamboo, another plant used for both food and building material.

Because there are thousands of miles of shoreline and abundant fresh water inland, Southeast Asians rely on fish and shellfish for a major part of their diet. Fresh and processed seafood are eaten in some form every day by most Southeast Asians. In some areas, they appear at virtually every meal.

To the outside world the greatest wealth of the region has been not in

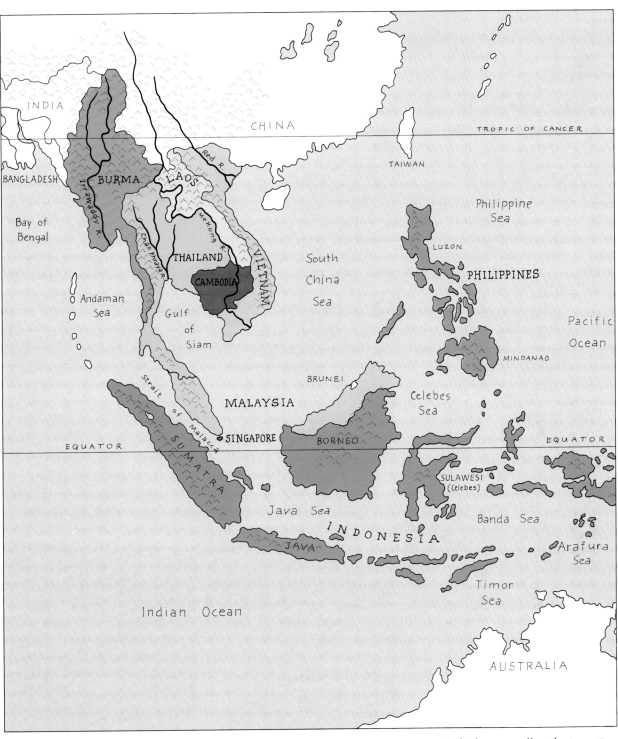

the staples of life, but in luxury items, particularly spices. For thousands of years, traders from around the world have come to the Indies for the spices native to these islands. The trading posts and colonies founded for the spice trade also became shipping points for other nonfood resources, including teak, rubber, tin, and other minerals, and most recently oil.

A LEGACY OF COMMERCE AND CONQUEST

The history of Southeast Asia is one of waxing and waning kingdoms and of repeated waves of outside conquests with their accompanying cultural influences. Archaeological evidence suggests that prehistoric Southeast Asia gave as much or more to the outside world as it received. These gifts include the cultivation of rice and other food plants and the first domestication of the familiar back-

yard chicken, as well as the invention of certain pottery and tool-making techniques. This cultural commerce worked both ways, and over the centuries, the region has absorbed influences from India, China, the Arab world, and Europe.

The underlying culture of much of Southeast Asia is Indian in origin. Some 2,000 years ago, most of the indigenous inhabitants belonged to two major ethno-linguistic groups:

the Malay, ancestors of most modern Malaysians, Indonesians, and Filipinos; and the Mon-Khmer, whose descendants live in present-day Burma and Cambodia. By the time of Christ, Indian missionaries had begun spreading Indian culture and Buddhism throughout the region, and their influence can still be seen in art, architecture, and alphabets. Over the next thousand years, immigrants arrived from the north, including the T'ai of southwestern China, ancestors of the Thai and Lao people of today. In the eleventh and twelfth centuries, the Indianized Khmer civilization reached its peak, dominating not only present-day Cambodia but also most of Thailand and parts of Laos and Vietnam. In the following centuries the Thai (Siamese), Lao, and Dai Viet kingdoms expanded at the expense of the Khmer, and the map of mainland Southeast Asia began to resemble its modern form.

Farther south, Arab spice traders had visited the Malay Peninsula and the islands of present-day Indonesia for hundreds of years before spreading Islam throughout the region beginning in the twelfth century. Foods flavored with mixtures of ground spices are found throughout the Moslem world, from Indonesia through northern India, from the Middle East to North Africa. Although many of these spices are indigenous to the Far East, their particular uses represent a mingling of cultures. Food habits undoubtedly migrated in both directions.

The next wave of conquest of Southeast Asia came from Europe, beginning late in the fifteenth century. Since the time of Rome, the spices of Southeast Asia had made their way to Europe via the markets of the Middle East, becoming fabulously expensive along the way. In 1498 the Portuguese, seeking to eliminate the Arab middlemen, found their way around Africa to the Indian Ocean and began to ship their own spices. Other Europeans followed, and the period of European colonialism in Asia began. The Dutch soon controlled Indonesia; the British, Burma and Malaya; and the Spanish, the

Philippines. France joined the colonial movement rather late, taking over Indochina (now the countries of Laos, Cambodia, and Vietnam) in the mid-nineteenth century.

During the colonial period, Europeans introduced many foods that became important ingredients in the cuisines we know today. Chiles, peanuts, squash, potatoes, sweet potatoes, tomatoes, and corn were all unknown in Asia until the European discovery of the Americas. The Portuguese and Spanish brought these foods home to Europe; they and the Dutch introduced them in turn to Southeast Asia, where they have become staples. The Dutch also brought Western varieties of cabbage, green beans, broccoli, and cauliflower to Indonesia and introduced coffee, now an important commercial crop.

The Chinese were always present in and around Southeast Asia as traders, often settling in port cities. They brought many culinary influences, such as stir-frying, and the various soybean-based foods, including soy sauce, tofu, and fermented bean sauces. In the nineteenth century the British brought large numbers of Chinese laborers to the Malay Peninsula. Periodic political upheavals and economic problems in China caused many more Chinese to emigrate. Today there are substantial Chinese populations in most cities of Southeast Asia, and Chinese food has had a widespread impact on most cuisines.

MEALS AND MENUS

A typical Southeast Asian meal consists of a generous portion of rice (or sometimes noodles), a smaller quantity of vegetables or fruit, and a still smaller amount of seafood, poultry, or meat. The dishes that accompany rice often combine vegetables and meats, much as is done in Chinese cooking.

Many Southeast Asian dishes are highly seasoned with chile and spices, and some of the favorite condiments are incendiary. Tolerance for hot flavors varies from person to person,

and the more chiles you eat, the more heat you can handle. Even so, many Westerners do not realize that these hot dishes are meant to be taken in small portions with a lot of rice. A curry that serves two people in a Thai restaurant here might serve four to six in Bangkok; and although patrons here might not finish even one bowl of rice, their Thai counterparts are likely to have several refills. As a result, many restaurateurs here tone down their dishes to suit what they view as Western tastes.

Most meals consist of several dishes, but they are not served as separate courses. Instead all are placed on the table at once, and diners help themselves to a little bit of each dish. The menu usually includes one or more sauces and condiments for seasoning dishes to taste. Soup is sipped throughout the meal, serving as both a beverage and another dish.

As a result of this pattern of serving, or perhaps because of the tropical heat, there is little concern about keeping hot foods hot. In fact about the only foods normally served piping hot are soups, which are often kept warm over a tabletop burner (see page 60). When rice is served hot, it is usually served in a covered container to keep it warm; but there are many occasions when rice is served at room temperature (see Rice Packets, page 104). At the other extreme only iced drinks and an occasional dessert are served quite cold. Salads are typically served on the cool side of room temperature, and curries and other foods that we would classify as hot dishes may be scarcely warmer than room temperature. Of course room temperature in the tropics may be close to 100° F, making really hot foods less desirable.

Perhaps the most famous form of Southeast Asian menu is the classic Indonesian rice table, better known by its Dutch name, *rijsttafel*. The Dutch colonial landowners took the traditional Indonesian meal of rice with a few accompanying dishes and turned it into an ostentatious display of wealth. In its most elaborate form, guests were seated at a long table, each with a plate of rice, while a parade of a dozen or more waiters filed past, each bearing a different item to be added to the diner's plate. The classic rijsttafel is out of fashion in modern-day Indonesia, being a reminder of colonial days, but it is still found in restaurants. Its modern equivalent is a more modest buffet, such as the menu on page 96, that still combines rice with an assortment of milder and hotter dishes, condiments, and sauces.

The menus in this book give some examples of meals from various countries of Southeast Asia. In choosing your own menus, always start with rice, then add dishes that offer a variety of flavors, colors, and textures. Try for a balance: Offset hotter dishes with milder ones; serve salads as a refreshing counterpart to richly sauced dishes; offer crisp-textured raw vegetables alongside long-simmered foods. A good meal should balance the five basic flavors of Asian cooking—sweet, sour, salty, bitter, and hot. The exact amounts of each are a matter of taste, but a meal that leans too heavily on one or two elements to the exclusion of the others will lack balance.

Most of the recipes in this book are designed to feed four to six people as part of a meal of several dishes. In planning menus, allow approximately one dish per person. Some recipes are easily doubled to feed a larger group, but the more common Southeast Asian practice is to add additional, varied dishes if more people are expected.

Dessert is not normally part of a Southeast Asian meal, but restaurants both here and in Asia often feature desserts to suit the tastes of tourists. Sweets are more likely to be served between meals, with tea or coffee. An exception is the Philippine *merienda*, a custom borrowed from the Spanish of serving a substantial midafternoon spread of snacks (see page 122). Like the English high tea, this may amount to quite a substantial meal by itself and always includes a variety of sweets.

One dessert that can follow any Southeast Asian meal is fresh fruit. Another possiblity, especially good if following a meal hot with chiles, is a sweet iced drink such as one of those on page 20.

Lunch is generally a simple meal, often consisting of a plate of noodles or a small portion of a curry or stir-fried dish served over rice. But meal times are not strictly adhered to, and snacking is in order at any time of the day or night. The streets of a Southeast Asian city are paradise for street snackers. Wherever people gather, in the market, at a sporting event, or on a downtown sidewalk, you will find an assortment of portable stands, carts, and tiny storefronts selling saté (skewered grilled meats), stir-fried noodles, roasted sweet corn in season, and all manner of tropical fruits and juices.

THE SOUTHEAST ASIAN DIET AND HEALTH

For the past decade or so, Western nutritionists have been advocating a diet low in meats, fats, and refined carbohydrates and high in seafood and the complex carbohydrates found in vegetables, fruits, and starches. These experts are describing a diet very much like that of Southeast Asia. With its reliance on rice and vegetables, the Asian diet provides plenty of complex carbohydrates. Cooking vegetables lightly or serving them raw preserves more of their nutritional value than does boiling them endlessly. Because meat has always been expensive in Asia, meat dishes are designed to make a little go a long way.

The overall amount of fat in the Southeast Asian diet is moderate compared to that of the West, and most of it comes from vegetable sources. Meats are typically leaner than ours and trimmed of most of their fat before cooking. Butterfat is not widely used. And despite the fact that coconut milk contains the most saturated of all vegetable fats, the health problems associated with high saturated-fat consumption (heart disease and

obesity) are relatively rare among Southeast Asians. One reason may be the traditional balance of the diet—lots of rice, small amounts of other foods. Recent research suggests another reason: There is increasing evidence that the type of fats found in fish and shellfish, so important in the Southeast Asian diet, actually reduces the harmful effects of saturated fats in the bloodstream.

If you are concerned with minimizing fats in your diet, do not include too many dishes based on coconut milk in a single meal, and make your own coconut milk when possible (see recipe page 38), as the homemade version tends to be less rich than the canned variety. When oil is called for, use an unsaturated vegetable oil such as corn or peanut rather than those containing coconut or palm oils (see Oils, page 29).

To those concerned with the amount of salt in their diets, some Southeast Asian foods may seem excessively salty. Fish sauce, soy sauce, and various other condiments do contain a lot of salt, but they are generally used in small quantities and provide the only source of salt in a dish. Bear in mind that rice is always cooked without salt. Taken as a whole a Southeast Asian meal need not contain any more salt than does a Western meal and may, in fact, have less.

Curries, grilled dishes, salads, and fiery condiments surround a heaping bowl of rice in the classic Indonesian rijsttafel or rice-table buffet (see page 8).

Chinese in origin, the wok is popular all over Southeast Asia for frying, stir-frying, and making curries and other stewed dishes. Essential wok accessories include a shallow ladle, a specially shaped spatula, and a wire skimmer. Also useful are a narrow-spouted oilcan, cooking chopsticks, and a cleaning brush.

TOOLS AND EQUIPMENT

Southeast Asian cooking requires little in the way of specialized tools and equipment. The recipes in this book can be prepared with the pots, pans, and other equipment found in a typical home kitchen. However, there are certain traditional designs that have been perfected over thousands of years.

THE WOK

One of the most pervasive examples of the Chinese influence in Southeast Asia is found in nearly every kitchen in the region: a round-bottomed cooking pan similar or identical to a Chinese wok. In Indonesia and Malaysia, it is known as a *kwali;* in the Philippines, *carajay;* and in Vietnam, *chao.* Some versions are shallower, some deeper; some have one handle, some two; they may be made of cast iron or aluminum or rolled steel; but all are clearly related to the Chinese original.

It is hard to imagine a more versatile or better designed piece of cookware than a wok. Its round bottom allows foods to be stir-fried or deep-fried with a minimum of oil. A steel or cast iron wok is an excellent conductor of heat, making it possible to cook over a very small fire. With a cover and a steaming rack or basket, the wok becomes a steamer for anything from bite-sized snacks to whole birds and fish. In this one pan, you can prepare a thick Thai curry, a zesty Vietnamese stir-fry, a fragrant Indonesian soup, or a Philippine noodle dish.

Selecting a Wok Woks are available in many designs and materials. The traditional shape is round bottomed for cooking over a gas flame (originally a charcoal brazier). Cooks with electric ranges should use a flat-bottomed wok for more efficient heating. A wok may have two metal-loop or two wood-trimmed handles, or one long wooden handle with or without a handle on the opposite side. A long handle is useful, especially for stir-frying, because it allows you to pour the contents out onto the serving platter more easily.

The best material for a wok is 14-gauge spun steel, about $5/64$ inch thick. This steel is light enough for easy handling, but heavy enough to conduct heat well. Cast iron is also traditional, but many home cooks find it too heavy. Other materials have definite disadavantages. Nonstick surfaces may be easier to clean, but they do not allow foods to brown as well as do steel or iron surfaces. Stainless steel is pretty, but it conducts heat poorly and is notorious for causing foods to stick. Gray anodized aluminum performs well but is very expensive.

Woks come in all sizes from 12 to 30 inches in diameter. The 14-inch size is the most common for home use and is included in the standard wok sets sold in most cookware and department stores. This size is a good compromise, especially if you have only one wok. However, if your stovetop space permits, a 16-inch or larger wok will make it much easier to cook a whole fish or large chicken. An ideal home set would include a 16-inch round-bottomed wok with metal handles (for cooking large items and frying in quantity) and a 12- or 14-inch long-handled wok (for most stir-fried dishes).

Among the essential wok accessories (included in most wok sets) are a wok ring; a cover; and a Chinese-style wire strainer, ladle, and spatula (see Hand Tools, at right). The ring, made of perforated metal, holds a round-bottomed wok steady over the fire. Some manufacturers of electric ranges now offer a replacement burner coil especially for round-bottomed woks, combining a ring with concave heating coils that match the shape of the wok. The cover should be a high dome, to accommodate large items such as steamed fish.

Optional wok accessories include steaming racks and bamboo steaming baskets (see Steamed Dishes, page 66), wire skimmers for fried foods (page 43), bamboo cleaning brushes, and long cooking chopsticks.

Seasoning a Wok Like a cast-iron skillet or griddle, a steel wok must be carefully maintained (seasoned) to give the best results. A well-seasoned wok can cook foods in the tiniest amount of oil without sticking, yet it grips the food during cooking for good browning in a way that no nonstick coated surface can.

Before using a brand-new wok, wash it well with detergent and a scouring pad to remove the protective coating of mineral oil. This should be the last time you wash it with detergent. Dry the wok well, then place it over a medium-high burner. When the metal has dried out thoroughly and a bluish haze appears in the middle, turn off the heat and pour 2 to 3 tablespoons cooking oil in a thin stream around the edge of the pan. Let the wok cool slightly, then rub the oil all over the inside with several thicknesses of paper towels. Rub until all the oil is absorbed and the towel picks up a gray stain from the metal. Heat again, add a little more oil, and wipe away the oil with

a clean paper towel. Repeat with 2 or 3 more coats of oil, or until the towel comes out clean.

Once the wok has been seasoned, the surface must be carefully maintained. After each use, wash it immediately with hot water. If any scrubbing is necessary, use a sponge, soft-bristled plastic brush, or plastic scrubbing pad, but never anything more abrasive. (The bamboo wok brushes sold with some wok sets don't work very well for this use.) Wipe dry, return to heat for a minute to dry further, and rub with a little oil. Eventually the wok will develop a thin black coating inside and out, and you will find its cooking qualities getting better and better.

Unfortunately some uses of the wok take away this carefully preserved finish. Dishes with a lot of liquid, such as many curries, tend to remove the film of oil that seals the surface. Steaming is especially hard on the finish. Whenever the wok is stripped of its seasoning by one of these methods or by neglect (such as leaving it full of water in the sink), it will have to be reseasoned. Deep-frying, on the other hand, is one of the best ways to build the coating back up. If storage space and budget permit, consider keeping one perfectly seasoned wok exclusively for stir-frying and another for all other cooking methods.

OTHER EQUIPMENT

Some Asian markets sell special steaming pans with perforated stacking trays, which rest on a large pot of water; these are handy for steaming large quantities of food or several different items at a time. See page 66 for more on steaming equipment.

The grilling recipes on pages 88 through 93 can be done with any standard home grill, from a small hibachi to a built-in barbecue. See page 88 for more on grilling equipment.

For all uses other than grilling or steaming, a standard selection of Western-style pots and pans will do. A heavy saucepan with a tight-fitting lid is ideal for cooking rice by the absorption method (see page 101). A large, lightweight pot is useful for making stocks and boiling noodles. Even a wok is not absolutely necessary; ordinary skillets and saucepans can cover all its functions, though perhaps less efficiently. A large skillet will do for stir-frying and pan-frying, and curries may be cooked in the same skillet, a saucepan, or a flame-proof casserole.

HAND TOOLS

Southeast Asian cooks make do with relatively few hand tools, most of them designed to be used with a wok. The wire strainer, a shallow basket of woven brass wire with a bamboo handle, is used to lift simmered foods out of their liquid or fried foods out of hot oil. The wok spatula is designed for maximum efficiency in stir-frying, its curved edge fitting into the curve of the wok. (A wooden spoon works fine for stirring curries and other slower-cooked dishes and does the job more quietly.) The shallow wok ladle can be used to add liquids to the wok, or it can be used in combination with the spatula, to scoop a finished mixture out onto a plate. Look for a ladle and spatula made of stainless steel; the more common rolled-steel variety must be carefully dried and oiled after each washing to prevent rust.

An oil can with a long, thin spout is handy for stir-frying. The narrow opening allows you to pour a tablespoon or two of oil in a thin stream around the edge of the wok, coating the sloping sides as it runs down into the center. The best ones come from China and Italy and are nearly identical in design. Don't buy too big a can, however, because it is not a good place for long storage of oil—the original can or bottle, tightly sealed, is better.

13

Basics

GRINDERS, GRATERS, AND BLENDERS

A mortar and pestle is as essential to a traditional Southeast Asian kitchen as is a stove. Ancient and simple in design, it is the best and most efficient tool for grinding spices and pounding aromatic ingredients into seasoning pastes. A curry paste made in a blender or food processor can never quite match the texture and flavor of one pounded by hand in a mortar. Although a mortar and pestle is not absolutely necessary to prepare authentic Southeast Asian dishes, it produces better results and is worth the modest investment.

Look for a mortar that is large, sturdy, and heavy. It should have a capacity of at least 1½ cups to efficiently pound a ½-cup mixture. The ideal type, sold in Southeast Asian, Indian, and some Latin American markets, is made of a fine-textured gray volcanic stone and comes with either a stone or a wooden pestle.

In addition to using a mortar and pestle to make sauces and curry pastes, you can use it to grind whole spices such as coriander seed or peppercorn, pound dried shrimp to a fluffy powder for topping salads, and grind peanuts or macadamia nuts to

a paste for thickening sauces. Ginger and galangal may also be grated with a box grater before pounding.

Blenders and food processors have replaced mortars and pestles in many modern Southeast Asian kitchens; both do an excellent job of grinding coconut for coconut milk (see page 38) and making acceptable curry pastes (see page 72). A food processor is handy for bulk shredding or slicing of vegetables. With the chopping blade it can grind meats or seafood for stir-fries, stuffings, or smooth fish pastes. A blender can also chop meats, though less efficiently.

There are some things neither machine can do as well as a knife can, such as chopping ginger for stir-fried dishes. Instead of cutting the ginger into discrete little bits, the machine smashes and tears it, ruining the texture and spraying the aromatic juice all over the inside of the work bowl. Garlic, shallots, and green onions are also better cut by hand than by machine.

Whether you use a food processor, blender, or mortar and pestle, a separate spice grinder is useful. Hand-cranked spice mills do a good job of grinding peppercorns and seeds, but they have a harder time with cinnamon sticks or dried galangal slices. Electric coffee grinders can handle all these items quickly and efficiently, and they are not much more expensive than the hand-crank type.

TABLEWARE

Table settings for Southeast Asian meals vary from one country to another, and within each country according to location and class. However, eating styles can be divided into three main categories: chopsticks, flatware, and fingers.

It is a common misconception among Westerners that all Asian foods are eaten with chopsticks. Most Southeast Asian restaurants in this country reinforce the notion, routinely offering their customers chopsticks because they think it is expected. However, eating with chopsticks is confined mainly to Vietnam and the Chinese communities of most Southeast Asian cities.

Where chopsticks are the norm, the rest of the table setting tends to follow the Chinese pattern: individual bowls for rice or noodles, smaller bowls and spoons for soup, shallow dishes for dipping sauces, and small plates mainly for bones and shells. Food is served in various bowls and platters with serving spoons, but in an informal setting, the diners help themselves to a morsel at a time with their chopsticks.

Spoons and forks are a relatively new addition to the Southeast Asian table, but their use is well established, especially in the cities. Knives are not part of table settings, the food is cut into bite-sized pieces in the kitchen. In this method of eating, the spoon is the main utensil, held in the right hand; the fork, held European-style in the left hand, is used to push food onto the spoon. Diners eat from large plates, with rice heaped in the center and small portions of various dishes around the outside. Although eating with spoon and fork may seem strange at first, it quickly becomes a comfortable and natural way to eat, especially for a typical meal of a lot of rice with several spicy and saucy additions.

In many parts of the region, food is most often eaten with fingers, with either rice or edible leaves acting as the spoon. Rice is often eaten in the same manner as Moroccan couscous: A tablespoonful or so of rice grains are lightly kneaded into a ball, dredged in a sauce, and popped into the mouth with just the first few fingers of one hand. Among Moslems, only the right hand is used. However, this style of eating is not limited to the Moslems of Indonesia and Malaysia; it is equally common among the Buddhist Lao and Burmese. Other foods are typically wrapped in a lettuce leaf or other edible wrapper such as rice paper (see page 118), dipped in a sauce, and eaten without cutlery. Saté meats and other foods on skewers are also natural dishes for eating with fingers.

When serving foods to be eaten with fingers, you might want to set individual finger bowls. To be authentic, float a jasmine or citrus blossom in each bowl, or use a sort of cooled tea made by steeping dried lime leaves in hot water. It is also traditional to pass warm, moist cloths (often infused with flower essences) before and after the meal.

There is no need to be too rigid about the type of tableware you use. When Thais order a dish of noodles from a sidewalk stand or go to a Chinese restaurant, they are perfectly comfortable eating with chopsticks. Many families that usually eat with fork and spoon use fingers for certain traditional dishes. Just relax and use whichever method feels most comfortable, and encourage your guests to do the same.

A normal Western assortment of plates, bowls, and serving dishes will cover all your needs for the foods in this book. If you want to be more authentic, Asian markets carry various traditional serving pieces, such as intricately decorated aluminum covered rice dishes from Thailand (see photo, page 100). You can also expand your range of serving dishes by lining shallow baskets or wooden trays with bamboo leaves. In fact, leaf-lined baskets are the most common form of serving dishes in much of the countryside.

Southeast Asian tableware often follows the Chinese pattern, except that spoons and forks are more common than chopsticks. Polished bronze flatware is a specialty of Thailand.

KNIVES

Three basic types of knives will cover nearly any cutting task in Southeast Asian cooking: a large-bladed vegetable knife, a heavy cleaver, and a small-bladed paring or utility knife. Either Western- or Asian-style knives will do.

Because of their large rectangular blades, which look vaguely like those of Western meat cleavers, all Chinese knives from lightweight vegetable knives to extra-heavy, bone-chopping cleavers tend to be lumped together under the name Chinese cleaver. But the name is misleading; only the heaviest of these knives are cleavers in the Western sense—that is, knives built to chop through bones. Look for a number from 1 to 5 imprinted on the blade; the higher the number, the smaller and lighter the knife. A number 1 knife can be used as a true cleaver, but the lighter versions are strictly for cutting up vegetables and boneless meats.

The Vegetable Knife

Unless otherwise specified, the cutting instructions throughout this book are for a vegetable knife. This can be either a medium-weight (number 3 or 4) Chinese knife, the similar but narrower-bladed Japanese type, or a French chef's knife. Whichever you choose, a stainless steel blade is ideal, since some ingredients will stain a carbon-steel blade. Choose the size that feels most comfortable, but if in doubt, go with a larger knife; with practice you will find the extra size and weight working for you.

Although a large vegetable knife may feel unwieldy at first, you will soon find it indispensable. It is good for slicing, dicing, and mincing, and its broad side can smash garlic or lemongrass. The blade is also handy for scooping up whatever you have just cut, from a bit of minced ginger to a pile of sliced cabbage, and transferring it to a bowl or wok.

The Cleaver

For cutting meats and poultry through the bone, you need a heavier, sturdier blade than for vegetables. Choose a number 1 knife or a heavier, thicker-bladed cleaver with no number on the blade. Heavy cleavers are ground differently than are vegetable knives. The blade of a vegetable knife is flat ground, with a constant taper from the top to the cutting edge; the cleaver blade tapers slowly from the top to within an inch or so of the edge, then tapers quickly to the cutting edge. The result is an edge that is not as fine as that on a vegetable knife but that is capable of hacking through bones without denting or cracking. A cleaver can be used for coarse chopping of meats and vegetables, but its bulkier blade makes thin slicing more difficult.

The Paring Knife

Some cutting tasks, such as peeling ginger, deveining shrimp, and making fancy decorative cuts, require a smaller, lighter knife. A Western-style paring knife is ideal. Just because this is a small knife, don't try to save money by buying an inexpensive one; a good paring knife from a reputable German, French, or American manufacturer will probably cost as much as a large Chinese vegetable knife. It will be worth every penny of the cost, as it will take and hold an edge better than a cheap knife.

Sharpening

A sharp edge is an absolute necessity and not only for good cutting. It is also a matter of safety; one of the easiest ways to cut yourself is by trying to force a cut with a dull knife.

The easiest and best way to maintain a sharp edge on any knife, Chinese or Western, is with a sharpening steel. If you don't already use a steel, learn to. It will save you time, money, and frustration. The ideal steel is at least 12 inches long, not counting the handle, with a smooth or very finely ridged surface. The steel does not remove any metal from the edge, as a whetstone does; rather it realigns the cutting edge to keep it

razor sharp. Sharpen your knife on the steel every time you use it, and it will hardly ever need to be sharpened on a stone or reground.

Hold the steel either out in front of you at chest level or vertically with the tip resting on the cutting board. Place the heel of the blade against the steel near the top, with the blade making an angle of 15 to 20 degrees. Maintaining gentle sideways pressure against the steel, swing the blade downward, drawing the cutting edge across the steel. Repeat on the other side of the steel. Alternate sides, making 10 or 12 strokes in all.

Cutting Surfaces

Because this cuisine requires so much chopping, slicing, and mincing, the cutting surface is almost as important as the knife. The cutting surface must be soft enough to cushion the edge of the blade so that it will not dull the knife, but hard enough to resist splintering or otherwise disintegrating into the food. Wood is the favorite cutting surface of most cooks. Laminated hardwood cutting boards and end-grain butcher blocks are both excellent choices.

Wood boards have some disadvantages. They require a lot of care, including periodic scraping and reoiling. They also tend to absorb food odors, and are harder to sterilize and deodorize than are nonporous materials. For these reasons, some cooks prefer a synthetic cutting surface for cutting up meats, poultry, and especially seafood. The best synthetic boards are made of a dense, opaque white polycarbonate and have a slightly uneven surface that gives under the knife. They are easy to clean with dishwashing detergent (which should never be used on a wood board). Do not confuse these boards with decorative boards of shiny plastic or other hard surface.

Whether you use a wood or synthetic cutting board, choose the largest size that will fit your work space. Nothing is more frustrating than trying to cut many things on a tiny cutting board.

CUTTING TECHNIQUES

Most of the following techniques are illustrated with a Chinese vegetable knife, but a French chef's knife or Japanese vegetable knife will also work just as well.

Work slowly at first until you get the hang of each technique; speed will come naturally. The important thing is to learn safe and efficient cutting habits. Give yourself plenty of room to work, stand in a comfortable position, relax, and focus entirely on the task at hand and you will find yourself cutting quickly and with minimum effort.

Hand Position

Holding food for safe and precise cutting is mostly a matter of keeping your fingers out of the way of the blade. For most cutting tasks, this means holding the food against the board with the fingertips curled back away from the blade. The blade then rides against the curved knuckles to guide the cut. As long as you do not lift the blade above the level of the knuckles and do not straighten out your fingers, there is no way that you can cut yourself in this position.

The position of the cutting hand depends upon the task. For precise cutting, grip the handle close to the blade, with the thumb and forefinger grasping the blade itself. There are two basic blade positions: Either rest the tip of the knife on the board and slice with a rocking motion, or lift the entire blade and, holding the edge parallel to the board, slice with a downward and forward motion. The former method allows more control, the latter more speed.

Slicing

Whether making thick or thin slices, crosswise or diagonal, the procedure is the same. Hold the food with the fingers curled back and the knuckles one slice-thickness back from the edge. Slice, using the knuckles to guide the blade, then move the fingers back along the food, or push the food forward with the thumb, to get into position for the next slice.

Shredding and Julienne Cutting

To cut food into fine shreds or larger matchsticks, first cut the ingredient into slices of the desired length and thickness. Carrots and other slender vegetables may have to be slant-sliced to achieve the right length. Stack the slices, overlapped slightly like shingles, and slice down through the stack lengthwise into sticks, square in cross section. Shreds are very fine julienne pieces, about 1/16 inch thick; matchsticks are twice as thick.

When slicing or shredding ginger or galangal, be sure to slice first across the grain; otherwise the pieces may be unpleasantly fibrous. To shred green onions, first slice them into the desired length. Slit the white and pale green sections lengthwise, but do not cut all the way through. Open the halves like a book and cut lengthwise into thin shreds. To shred the hollow green tops, bundle them together under the fingertips of the food-holding hand and carefully slice the bundle.

Dicing and Mincing

These two terms refer to the same process, but differ in the size of the cut. "Diced" means cut into cubes of 1/4 to 1/2 inch; "minced," about 1/16 inch; and "finely diced" somewhere in between. First cut the ingredient you are preparing into shreds or matchsticks of the desired thickness as described above. Then gather the sticks into a bundle and cut across into uniform cubes.

Garlic, onion, and shallot are minced by a slightly different method. First, peel, leaving root end intact, then split in half lengthwise. Place cut side down on board. Holding knife horizontally, make one or more cuts parallel to cutting board, almost to root end. Next make a series of vertical lengthwise cuts of the desired thickness. Then slice across the cuts working toward the root end to produce cubes. Discard root end.

Smashing and Bruising

When an aromatic ingredient such as garlic, ginger, green onion, or lemongrass is used in large pieces to flavor a dish, bruising or smashing it first helps release its flavors into the food. Cut to the desired size, place pieces on the board, and smack them smartly with the broad side of the blade. Another method is to place the knife flat on top, then pound it with your fist. If you use this technique, watch out for the cutting edge.

Chopping

Sometimes uniform cubes are not necessary. For example, in making curry pastes, it will speed up the process to cut the harder ingredients into smaller sizes before adding them to the mortar or blender. Place a pile of peeled garlic cloves or ginger slices on a board. Grip the knife a little farther out on the handle than for slicing. Use the other hand to press the tip of the knife down against the board and chop with a rocking motion, pivoting the knife back and forth over the food. Chop to the desired size, scraping the pile together occasionally.

Cleaver Chopping

Using a cleaver or a heavy vegetable knife, it is easy to chop meats to any texture from rough cubes to a fine paste. Start by dicing the meat, then change to a chopping grip (knife hand well back on the handle, thumb on top or on side). Swing from the wrist for maximum chopping efficiency. With a good heavy cleaver, not much downward force is really necessary—it is more a matter of lifting the knife and letting it fall. The other hand is not involved in this type of chopping. Stop every once in a while to scrape the pile of pieces back together.

To chop through bones, as in cutting a chicken into braising pieces, hold the knife as above. However, it may be necessary to hold the food with the other hand. For safety's sake, hold the food as far away from where you will cut as possible. When you get to the last couple of inches, just place the food on the board, get your other hand out of the way, take aim, and chop.

CUTTING UP POULTRY

Here are the basic techniques for disjointing a chicken or duck, boning the breast, and cutting up the whole bird, bones and all, into bite-sized sections known as curry pieces or braising pieces.

Disjointing

Chicken may be disjointed with a Chinese cleaver or a boning knife. The following steps also apply to whole ducks or any other poultry, from squab to turkey.

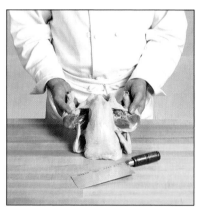

1. Pick up chicken with both hands, breast side up. Spread legs outward to pop hip joints free.

2. Cut through skin between leg and breast. Turn chicken on its side and cut leg free along with meat from back. (If you plan to use the back in the dish that you are preparing, leave more meat attached.) Pull wing away from body and cut away from breast, being careful not to cut too deeply into breast meat. Repeat with other leg and wing.

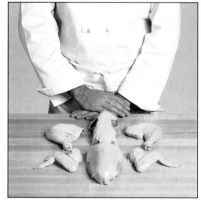

3. Hold chicken by tip of breastbone and cut through ribs to separate breast from back. Pull or chop breast free from back at base of wishbone.

Boning the Breast

In Southeast Asian cooking, poultry is usually cooked with the bones for more flavor. But boned breast meat is used, particularly in stir-fried dishes.

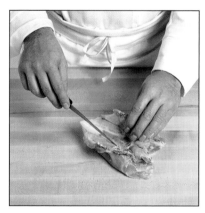

1. Remove skin. Place breast skin side down. With tip of knife, cut through thin membrane covering breastbone.

2. Pick up breast with both hands and press back on ribs to break them away from breastbone, which will pop out. Pull out breastbone, including cartilage.

3. With short cuts using tip of knife, cut away ribs as close to bone as possible. Or slip fingers between ribs and meat and work meat free from bones. Work wishbone free with fingers or cut out with tip of knife.

4. Split breast in half, removing tough membranes lying along breastbone. Locate white tendon on smaller muscle of each half. Place tendon side down on board and hold end with a fingernail. With knife held vertically, scrape from end of tendon inward, removing meat from tendon.

Cutting For Braising

To cut a chicken into braising pieces (1 to 2 inches with bones), first disjoint the bird as instructed on opposite page. Remove excess fat from the cavity and neck area. Remove the kidneys, the spongy organs along backbone near tail end. Rinse well.

1. Hold a leg by the end of the drumstick, as far from cutting point as possible. Lift cleaver a foot or so above cutting board and chop down through thigh bone with a firm, decisive blow. The knife should cut cleanly through the bone without shattering it. Cut thigh and drumstick into two or three pieces each. Hold wings by tips and cut upper and middle joints into two pieces each. Leave tip whole, for decoration.

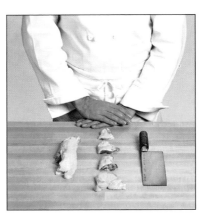

2. Split breast in half lengthwise, then chop each half into three or four pieces with skin attached. Chop along one side of backbone to split back in half; leave backbone attached to other side. Chop each back half crosswise into four or five pieces.

PREPARING A WHOLE FISH

Like poultry, fish retains its flavor and moisture better if cooked whole, with the bones. To prepare a whole fish for frying or steaming, follow these steps.

1. Have fish cleaned and scaled, with head and tail left on. Cut open belly cavity, if this was not done in cleaning. Pull away any bits of gills and internal organs. Look for two strips of red tissue lying alongside backbone; if present, cut them open with tip of knife. Rinse cavity well under running water until no trace of bloody tissue remains.

2. Score both sides of fish with diagonal cuts almost to the bone, 1 to 2 inches apart. This speeds the cooking time and allows the seasonings to penetrate the fish faster. If you want to serve a steamed or fried fish "swimming" on the platter (belly side down), cut back from cavity toward tail on one side of bones, extending the cavity toward the tail. Spread the rib cage open and arrange the fish upright on the steaming plate, bending the tail to fit, if necessary. See Fried Whole Fish, Nonya Style, page 44.

WHAT TO DRINK WITH SOUTHEAST ASIAN FOOD

In most Asian restaurants in this country, a pot of tea automatically lands on the table along with the menus. This may lead Westerners to assume that tea is the usual drink with Southeast Asian meals. However, tea is not always served with meals, nor is it the only drink that goes well with Southeast Asian foods.

When hot tea is served at the table, it is more likely to be a weak jasmine tea than a full-flavored variety. Stronger teas are generally served between meals. Iced tea, on the other hand, is popular at mealtime.

East and West, beer is a popular drink to accompany highly seasoned foods (see photograph opposite, back). A well-chilled lager does a good job of putting out the fire when you eat a bit too much chile. The Thai Singha brand and the Philippine San Miguel brand are among the best known Southeast Asian beers.

Wine is difficult to match with most Southeast Asian foods, except for the mildest dishes. A complex curry full of chiles, galangal, garlic, and shrimp paste will overwhelm most delicate wines, and stronger-flavored wines may end up fighting for attention. If you want to try wine, stick to a medium-dry or slightly sweet white wine, one that will serve more as a refreshment than as a flavor complement to the food.

Indonesia produces some of the world's finest coffees, not only the famous Java but also coffees from Sumatra and Sulawesi (Celebes). In Vietnam and Cambodia, coffee is brewed strong and dark and served with sweet milk (see recipe at right). A similar Thai version uses coffee flavored with vanilla.

Carbonated soft drinks, another Western import, are extremely popular in Southeast Asia. Like a cold beer or a glass of fruit juice, they can be a refreshing antidote to an overdose of chile. Unfortunately, most are far too sweet. A better nonalcoholic alternative is sparkling water or club soda with fruit juice added to taste (see photo opposite, right). Iced Lemongrass Tea, below, is another caffeine-free choice. Plain iced water is probably the most popular and refreshing drink of all.

THAI ICED TEA
Cha thai

This drink requires a unique tea from northern Thailand, sold in Asian markets as *cha thai*. At first glance it looks more like ground coffee than tea; the leaves are finely chopped and flavored with vanilla and roasted corn, and artificial color is added to boost its naturally red color. It is traditionally brewed in a cloth bag. Hot water is poured through the bag several times, producing a stronger brew each time. A drip-coffee cone and filter make a fine substitute. When milk is added, the tea turns a striking brick-orange color (see photograph opposite, center back).

> *Thai tea (cha thai), 2 to 3 tablespoons per serving*
> *Boiling water, about 6 ounces per serving*
> *Sugar or sweetened condensed milk, to taste*
> *Milk or half-and-half*

1. Place tea in a coffee filter in a drip cone. Preheat carafe with boiling water; discard water. Pour 6 ounces boiling water per serving into cone and let it drip through. Transfer brew to another container, then pour back through filter. Repeat until tea is deep red in color, a total of 4 to 6 times.

2. Sweeten tea to taste with sugar or condensed milk. Fill tall glasses with ice cubes and add tea to fill glasses halfway. Add milk or half-and-half and stir.

Variation The tea may be brewed in a teapot, but it will still need to be filtered through a paper filter or a very fine nylon strainer. Preheat pot with boiling water and allow to steep 6 to 8 minutes before straining.

VIETNAMESE COFFEE

In restaurants and cafés, dark-roast coffee is brewed in an individual drip pot that sits on top of a glass, slowly dripping into sweet milk (see photograph opposite, center front). It takes a good 10 to 15 minutes for the water to finish dripping through, and the coffee is sipped at an equally leisurely pace. Both the coffee and the pots are available in Southeast Asian markets, but any type of coffee and any brewing method that produces a strong, rich-tasting cup will do.

> *1 to 2 tablespoons sweetened condensed milk, at room temperature*
> *4 to 6 ounces strong, dark brewed coffee*

Place the milk in the bottom of an 8-ounce glass. Carefully pour in coffee, trying not to disturb the layer of milk. Stir milk up from bottom and sip coffee. There will probably be some milk left in the bottom of the glass when you are finished.

Makes 1 serving.

Variation This coffee may also be served iced. Add ice cubes on top of the sweet milk and proceed as above.

ICED LEMONGRASS TEA

Flakes of dried lemongrass are sold in natural food stores and herb shops. If you grow your own (see page 28), this is a good use for the tough, leafy tops. Adjust the sweetness of the tea (see photograph opposite, left) to taste, using a little more sugar if the accompanying foods are really hot.

> *¼ cup chopped fresh lemongrass tops or 2 tablespoons dried flakes*
> *4 cups boiling water*
> *Sugar, to taste*

Preheat teapot with boiling water; discard water. Add lemongrass and boiling water, steep 8 to 10 minutes; strain. Allow to cool, sweeten to taste, and serve in tall glasses with ice.

Serves 4.

Coconut, chile, and lemongrass are among the basic flavoring ingredients used over and over again throughout Southeast Asia.

Ingredients, Condiments & Sauces

The Asian cook, like fine cooks everywhere, relies on good basic ingredients. Here is a guide to the fresh ingredients and the various canned, dried, frozen, and preserved foods you will need to prepare authentic dishes from all over Southeast Asia. Tips on where to shop, including mail-order sources, are included on page 33. Here too you'll find recipes for basic condiments and sauces served at nearly every meal, such as the Vietnamese Nuoc Mam Sauce (see page 35) and the Indonesian Sambal Bajak (see page 37). A Special Feature on coconuts, an essential part of all Southeast Asian cooking, includes a recipe for making your own coconut milk (see page 38).

A GLOSSARY OF SOUTHEAST ASIAN INGREDIENTS

The exotic cuisines of Southeast Asia use some ingredients that are familiar to every supermarket shopper and others that seldom, if ever, reach these shores. But the growing number of Southeast Asian immigrants in the United States and the increasing popularity of Thai, Vietnamese, and Indonesian restaurants make it easier all the time to cook authentically flavored Southeast Asian dishes.

Wherever Southeast Asians settle there is bound to be at least one store that sells products from "back home." Southeast Asian farmers now living in the warmer parts of the United States are growing fresh vegetables and herbs that were scarce or unknown here just a few years ago. Hawaii in particular provides us with fresh tropical produce that would be prohibitively expensive to ship all the way from Asia. Southeast Asian restaurants offer another source, if not of ingredients, at least of advice on where to find them. If what you need is not available locally, try one of the mail-order sources listed on page 33.

Here is a guide to the most common Southeast Asian ingredients, all used in the recipes in this book. Variations in names found on product labels or in catalogs are given in parentheses.

Annatto (Achuete, Atsuete) This brick red seed is used in Philippine food mostly for the bright orange or yellow color it imparts; the flavor is oddly dusty and only vaguely spicy. The seeds, sold in Philippine and Latin American markets, are typically soaked in water or heated in oil, then discarded, and the oil or water is used to color the food. Philippine markets also sell a liquid annatto extract, which is easier to use.

Bamboo Shoots The edible shoots of large bamboo plants give crunch and a slightly sweet flavor to stir-fries and other dishes. They can sometimes be found fresh in Asian markets, and are also available in cans. Drain and discard the canning liquid before using. If a canned flavor persists, blanch the shoots in fresh water. Leftover shoots can be stored covered in the refrigerator, in fresh water, for a few days. Store them in another container, not in the can. Fresh whole bamboo shoots are sold in some Asian markets in buckets of water. Store them in water in the refrigerator for a few days, changing the water daily.

Banana Leaves These large, flat leaves are the aluminum foil, wrapping paper, and doily of Southeast Asia, used to wrap foods for cooking or storage and to line baskets and platters for serving. Frozen leaves are available in Asian and Latin American markets; once thawed, they will keep in the refrigerator for a few months. Foods cooked in banana leaves take on some flavor and color from the leaves, which is missing from the same foods cooked in foil.

Basil Several varieties of sweet basil are grown and used in Southeast Asia, particularly in Thailand. A purple-stemmed variety known as *horapa* or Thai basil is sometimes available here, but any fresh basil will do. Basil is easy to grow outdoors in summer or year round in an indoor window. Dried basil is a poor substitute; either do without or use fresh mint, which is close enough in flavor.

Bean Curd See Tofu.

Bean Sprouts Sprouted mung beans give a pleasant crunchy texture to many Asian dishes. (Some stores also carry soybean sprouts, which have larger seeds and require longer cooking.) Look for crisp, white sprouts with a fresh smell; avoid those with withered tails. Buy sprouts the same day you use them, if possible; otherwise blanch them for a few seconds in boiling water, rinse under cold water, and store in cold water in the refrigerator. Sprouts are easy to grow at home, and most health-food stores sell the beans and specially designed sprouting jars with instructions for their use.

Bean Threads Also known as cellophane noodles, glass noodles, and Chinese vermicelli, these very fine, semitransparent noodles are made from mung bean starch. Besides being used as noodles, they are added to stuffings (see Crab Rolls, page 119) and even to desserts. Asian markets sometimes sell them in bundles of small individual packages, a convenience that is well worth the slight extra cost. Bean threads are usually soaked in warm water before use and require no further cooking. They can, however, stand long simmering without becoming mushy as other noodles would, making them ideal for soups.

Black Mushrooms, Dried (Shiitake) Although they are not native to the region, dried Chinese mushrooms are widely used in Southeast Asian cooking. Commonly known by the Japanese name *shiitake,* they have a broad, flat cap, a short stem, and a fine meaty flavor. Asian markets carry several grades; the best have a lacy system of cracks on the surface of the brown cap, showing the creamy flesh underneath. Dried black mushrooms keep for months in a cool, dry place. To use soak them in warm water until soft, then drain; if the liquid is not used in the dish, save it for soups or stocks. The tough stems are usually discarded.

The fresh shiitake mushrooms now being raised commercially in this country do not have the depth of flavor of the imported dried variety and they should not be used as a substitute. They are very good, however, when used in place of fresh mushrooms in any of the recipes in this book.

Cabbage Both Asian and Western varieties of cabbage are common in Southeast Asia. The Dutch long ago introduced the familiar pale green type into Indonesia, where it is now a staple crop. The term "Chinese cabbage" covers several types native to Asia. One common variety, known in Western markets as Napa cabbage or celery cabbage, has a tight, cylindrical, pale green head with a mild flavor. The other major type, bok choy or *choy sum,* is slightly stonger in flavor. It has a loose head of deep green leaves with contrasting thick white stems. Some markets carry a smaller relative of bok choy that has greenish stems, known appropriately enough as baby bok choy. Recipes specify the type that is to be used.

Cardamom The seed pod of a tropical plant related to ginger, cardamom is an important spice in Southeast Asian cooking, particularly in curry pastes and other spice blends. Cardamom is available as whole white pods, about ⅓ inch long; as seeds, with the outer part of the pod removed; or ground into powder. For maximum flavor and aroma, buy the whole pods and shell and grind them just before using.

Chiles Southeast Asian cooking uses a variety of fresh and dried chiles, but they can be grouped roughly into two categories: hot and even hotter. Generally speaking, the smaller the chile, the hotter the flavor.

Fresh chiles are often used in their red (fully ripe) state. Fortunately ripe chiles are becoming more widely available in our markets. When a recipe specifies fresh red chiles, look for the red Fresno chile, about 3 inches long, 1 inch thick, and sharply tapered, or the red jalapeño, similar in length but a little thinner. These chiles are definitely hot, but the heat is reduced by removing the seeds and ribs. A milder alternative is the red-ripe Anaheim or New Mexico chile, generally used ribs and all.

For an even hotter flavor, use a small green chile such as the thin, 2-inch-long *serrano.* A few Asian markets carry tiny green or red Thai bird or bird's-eye chile. About an inch long on a long stem and almost all seeds, this variety is a leading contender for the world's hottest chile.

Store fresh chiles in the refrigerator, loosely wrapped in a paper towel inside a plastic bag. They will keep for several weeks this way, although they may lose some moisture. For longer storage, boil chiles for 3 minutes, cut off the stem end, wrap tightly, and freeze. The texture

SPELLING AND PRONUNCIATION

Trying to accurately render the sounds of the various languages of Southeast Asia into English is a complicated task. Many are based on alphabets other than Roman. Some are tonal; the same vowels have different sounds that give different meanings. And in most cases there is more than one system for transliterating each language into the Roman alphabet.

A detailed discussion of the spelling and pronunciation of Southeast Asian languages is beyond the scope of this book, but a few general rules are given here to point you toward correct pronunciation of the names of ingredients and dishes.

Vowels and diphthongs Except as otherwise noted below, these are similar to those of English: *a* as in *father,* not as in *play; e* as in *hen,* or when accented, like a long *a,* as in *able; i* as in *sit,* or like long *e,* as in *easy; o* as in *toe* or *long; u* as in *flute* or *put. Ai* is pronounced like long *i* as in *high; eo* as in *mayo.*

Consonants These are mostly similar to those of English; exceptions are noted below. *B, ch, d, f, l, m, n, p, r, s, t, v, w,* and *y* are virtually the same sounds as in English. *C* is usually pronounced hard, like *k,* except in Indonesia and Malaysia, where it is pronounced *ch. J* is pronounced as in English, except in older Indonesian spellings. Notes on specific languages follow. A few consonants are aspirated, that is, spoken with a little puff of air.

Indonesian and Malay Indonesia adopted a new official spelling system in 1972, and several older Dutch-based transliterations were changed to be consistent with more languages. Thus the capital *Djakarta* became *Jakarta; ajam* became *ayam; oelek* became *ulek;* and *ketjap* became *kecap* (pronounced *ketchup;* see Kecap Manis, page 28). However, the older spellings persist on many package labels. Malay words generally follow the same rules. However, English spelling of the *ch* sound varies; the word for shrimp paste may be spelled *blachan* or *belacan.*

Thai A tonal language with a Sanskrit-based alphabet, Thai is especially variable in its English spellings. There is no attempt in this book to represent the tones of vowels; just follow the rules above. *Ae* is pronounced like *cat, oe* like *fur* without the final *r,* and *oo* like either *foot* or *tooth.* Consonants do not exactly match those in English. The Thai name for the Kaffir lime may be spelled *makrut* or *makrud,* but the pronunciation is more or less *magroot,* the middle consonant sound falling somewhere between *g* and *k.* An initial consonant followed by *h* (*th, kh, ph*) indicates a harder, more aspirated sound than that of the single letter. When certain groups of consonants fall at the end of a word or syllable, they are pronounced in the same way. For example, *p, b, f,* and *ph* all sound like *p.* And *f, th, d, ch,* and *s* all sound like something between *t* and *d.* Both these final consonant sounds are softer than they would be if they came at the beginning of a syllable.

Vietnamese In authentic Vietnamese spelling, many vowels are accompanied by diacritical marks both above and below the letter. These accents do not appear in this book, and the use of Vietnamese names is kept to a minimum. Of the few Vietnamese words used here, the only one that might be troublesome to pronounce is the common word for "sauce," *nuoc,* pronounced *nyuk.*

An assortment of fresh ingredients used in Southeast Asian cooking includes, in basket (clockwise from top): eggplant, Chinese cabbage, fresh coriander, black mushrooms, Chinese long beans, and, in center, bean sprouts. Outside basket (clockwise from lower right) are ginger, green papaya, serrano chiles, galangal, lemongrass, and Chinese okra, a cucumberlike vegetable.

will suffer slightly, but the flavor will be fine for curry pastes or recipes calling for minced fresh chile. Another way to store them is in the form of sambal ulek (see page 37).

The ideal dried chile for Southeast Asian cooking is the ripened and dried version of the serrano. This is the familiar whole or flaked red pepper of spice racks, also known in Spanish as *chile japonés* or by the Japanese name *santaka*. Similar chiles are also grown in Asia, and they are apt to be least expensive when sold in bags in Asian markets. If you prefer a milder dried chile, use the larger red California or New Mexico chile, sold whole or ground in Latin American groceries.

Caution is necessary. Be careful in handling any chiles, fresh or dried. The flesh, seeds, and especially the ribs or veins contain an irritating substance called capsicin. Always wash your hands (and knives and other tools) thoroughly after handling chiles, and do not touch your eyes or other sensitive areas. If your

skin is especially sensitive, wear rubber or plastic gloves when handling chiles. Also, if you are chopping a quantity of chiles in a food processor or blender, do not hold your face over the container when you lift the lid; the fumes may irritate your eyes and nose.

Chile Sauce, Liquid Various prepared chile sauces are used in Southeast Asian cooking. Sriracha (also spelled Siracha) is popular, from Thailand, and available in several degrees of hotness. The hot version is similar to a Louisiana-style hot sauce, which can be substituted.

Chinese Beans Also known as long beans or yard-long beans, these have elongated pods (actually about 1½ feet) and are a little firmer and crunchier than regular green beans, making them excellent for curries and stir-fried dishes. They come in two colors, a pale green and a deeper green. Look for slender, smooth pods without enlarged seeds.

Chinese Sausage A firm, slender, slightly sweet sausage made mainly of pork liver, Chinese sausage is used in some Vietnamese and Philippine dishes. It is sold in packages, or loose in pairs tied together with string. Chinese sausage keeps well under refrigeration or frozen.

Cloud Ears This edible Chinese fungus is also known as tree ears, wood ears, and black fungus and is sometimes translated on package labels as dehydrated vegetable. Cloud ears are used mainly for their crunchy-gelatinous texture in dishes showing Chinese influence. The best type is sold in packages of small, irregular pieces less than an inch across, deep brown on top and medium brown on the underside. The other common form, which is much larger, black on top, and pale gray underneath, is also much tougher, even after soaking.

Coconut Cream See Special Feature, page 38.

Coconut Milk See Special Feature, page 38.

Coriander, Fresh Also known as cilantro and Chinese parsley, this distinctively flavored herb is widely used in Southeast Asia. It inspires extreme reactions. Those who like it cannot get enough of it, while others cannot even stand its smell. There is no substitute; if the herb is unavailable, or if you dislike the flavor, leave it out. (Coriander seed, although it comes from the same plant, has a completely different flavor from the fresh herb.) Fortunately fresh coriander is now widely available in this country, generally under the name cilantro. The leaves are used whole or chopped or pounded into seasoning mixtures. Stored with the roots in water and the tops loosely enclosed in a plastic bag, fresh coriander will keep for nearly a week.

Some Thai curry pastes call for coriander roots, and in Asian groceries the bunches often include an inch or more of root. If not enough root is present, chop the bases of the stems to make up the difference. If you grow your own, simply pull up the plants with the roots attached.

Coriander Seed A common spice found throughout the tropics, coriander seeds, which look like white peppercorns, have a mild, slightly lemony flavor and aroma. They are most frequently used ground up in curry pastes.

Cucumbers Raw cucumbers are frequently used in Southeast Asia, both in salads and as a crunchy accompaniment to cooked dishes. The waxy-skinned hothouse type should be peeled, and may be seeded before preparing if desired. The slender English or Japanese cucumbers, often sold individually wrapped, do not need peeling or seeding.

Cumin The special flavor and aroma of this cosmopolitan spice are familiar to lovers of Indian curries, Moroccan cooking, and Texas chili. In Southeast Asia, where it is mostly used in curries and similar spice blends, cumin is a sign of Indian influence. Toasting whole cumin seeds in a dry skillet just before grinding brings out their flavor.

Curry Leaves (Daun Kari, Neem) About the size of slender bay leaves, curry leaves have a mild sweet-spicy aroma. Dried neem from India is sold in small packages in Indian stores, but it often has little flavor; look for some with strong aroma. Fresh curry leaves are occasionally available from Florida, and they can be dried and kept in a jar for future use. Dried salam leaves (see page 29) are an acceptable substitute; or the curry leaves can be omitted.

Eggplant Several varieties of small eggplant are used in Southeast Asian cooking, a few of which are now being grown here. One type, commonly known as Thai eggplant, is green and white and about 1½ inches in diameter. Even smaller is the pea eggplant, about the size of the smallest cherry tomato. It is often eaten raw for its pleasantly bitter flavor.

Fish Sauce (Fish's Gravy, Nam Pla, Nuoc Mam, Patis) This salty brown liquid extract of fermented fish is used throughout Southeast Asia. The ubiquitous fish sauce, which tastes much better than it sounds, is basic to the dishes of the region, just as soy sauce is the base of so much of Chinese and Japanese cuisine. Like soy sauce, it provides not only salt and liquid, but also a versatile background to other flavors. Each country has its own version, but most of the fish sauce available here comes from Thailand; a little is imported from the Philippines, Singapore, and Hong Kong. Vietnamese cooks prefer the type made from anchovies, usually labeled *ca com*. Store fish sauce tightly sealed at room temperature.

Galangal (Laos, Ka) A close relative of ginger, galangal is common in Southeast Asian cuisines. Sometimes called aromatic ginger or Siamese ginger, galangal (*Alpinia galanga*) has a pronounced aroma and flavor—a little like ginger, but with medicinal, mustardlike overtones. In small quantities it gives an exotic flavor to curries and soups. Fresh galangal rhizomes grown in Hawaii are now available in well-stocked Asian markets in this country. The next best form is little packages of thick dried slices. Less desirable is the ground form often sold as laos powder (its Indonesian name, which has nothing to do with the country of Laos). Store fresh galangal in the same way as ginger (see below).

Ginger This is one of the essential flavors of all Asian cuisines. Sliced, minced, or grated, it gives a refreshingly clean, hot flavor to all kinds of foods, such as Steamed Fish With Ginger-Mushroom Sauce (see page 68). The familiar dried and ground ginger of spice racks is not a substitute; fortunately, fresh ginger rhizomes or "roots" are now widely available. Look for rock-hard rhizomes that snap easily into pieces. Fresh ginger will keep for a week or more in the refrigerator. For longer storage, wrap it in a paper towel first and store in a plastic bag. Change the paper as it absorbs moisture from the ginger or else mold will form.

Also called scallions, spring onions, or even shallots in some parts of the country, these slender immature onions are widely used in Asian cooking. Unless otherwise specified in a recipe, use both the white bottoms and the green tops.

Kaffir Lime (Makrut) The juice, rind, and leaves of this lime (*Citrus hystrix*) are used in Southeast Asian cooking for their flavor and aroma. The bumpy, dark green skin is minced or pounded into curry pastes; the tart juice is used in sauces and salad dressings; and the leaves are added whole or cut into shreds to soups and curries. Dried *makrut* peel and leaves from Thailand are available in Southeast Asian markets, and, as of this writing, it was being grown on an experimental basis in southern California. Fresh leaves are not currently available. Our variety of lime is similar enough in the flavor of the juice, but its peel is much thinner and is only a last-resort substitute for makrut. If you have access to any sort of citrus tree, its fresh leaves are preferable to the dried imported variety.

Kecap Manis This thick, sweetened soy sauce from Java, used in Indonesian cooking, gets its peculiar flavor from molasses. *Kecap*, a Malay-Indonesian word meaning seasoned sauce, is pronounced *ketchup* and is, in fact, the root of our word for the ubiquitous tomato condiment. One widely available brand of kecap manis is Conimex, which comes in both a spiced and a plain version and is labeled with the old spelling *ketjap*. A homemade version may be made with either Japanese-style soy sauce (such as the widely available Kikkoman brand) or a Chinese black soy sauce (see recipe, page 34).

Krachai (Rhizome) A rhizome of the ginger family, *krachai* (*Kaempferia pandurata*) resembles miniature ginger, but has thick fingerlike roots extending down from the rhizome. The flavor is somewhat similar to that of galangal, and the two can be used interchangeably. This is the mysterious ingredient known simply as rhizome in canned

Tips

GROWING YOUR OWN HERBS

Southeast Asian cooking uses relatively few herbs, but those few are almost indispensible, and the dried versions are not always satisfactory. If you do not have easy access to markets selling fresh basil, coriander, or lemongrass, you might try growing your own. All the following herbs will grow outdoors in warm weather, or indoors on a sunny windowsill in winter. For sources of seeds and plants, see Where to Shop for Southeast Asian Ingredients, page 33.

Basil A warm-season annual, basil comes in many varieties as well as the familar large-leafed kind used in Mediterranean cooking. Among these other varieties available through specialty seed catalogs are lemon basil (which is nearly identical to a Thai variety), anise basil (similar to the Thai *horapa*), and the attractive purple-leafed dark opal variety.

All the basils need full sun and warm temperatures. Where growing seasons are long, sow outdoors when the soil is warm; in shorter-season areas, sow indoors about six weeks before the last frost. They also grow well in sunny windows or under lamps. Pinch off flowers as they appear, to keep plants from going to seed and dying.

Coriander This herb grows easily from seed, the same seeds found in spice racks (although nursery seeds are more reliable). Coriander does not transplant well, so sow it where it will grow, either in the ground or in pots. Because the plants go to seed quickly, plant every few weeks for a steady supply.

Lemongrass Since lemongrass grows by spreading rather than from seed, it is easy to start with stalks bought for cooking. Stand a fresh stalk in a glass of water. When it sprouts roots and shoots, plant it in a sunny area. It will survive mild winters and tolerate some frost. Harvesting can begin after a few months. To harvest cut the largest stalks from the center at or just below the soil line, taking care not to cut adjacent stalks. Divide the clumps every year or so. Home-grown lemongrass is likely to be slimmer than the commercial variety, so use two stalks where a recipe calls for one.

Mint All varieties of mint are easy to grow as long as they get plenty of water (try it near a leaky faucet). Mint spreads by runners near the surface, so if you plan to plant it outdoors, you may want to contain it with boards sunk several inches into the soil.

Thai curry pastes. It is occasionally available fresh, but more commonly it comes in little bags of dried shreds, labeled "rhizome," with or without the Thai name krachai or kachai.

Lemongrass An essential herb in Southeast Asian cooking, lemongrass is a stiff, pale green, grassy plant, a foot or so tall, with a delightful lemony aroma. Now widely grown by Asian farmers in warmer areas of the United States, fresh lemongrass is generally available in Asian groceries. Dried lemongrass flakes (available in health-food stores) are an acceptable substitute, as is the powdered version sold in Asian markets.

To use fresh lemongrass, remove the outer leaves and slice thinly across the stem from the base up to where the leaves begin to separate. Most recipes call for the slices to be minced or pounded to a paste with other ingredients. Dried flakes should be ground in a spice grinder before adding them to pastes.

Lily Flowers The dried, unopened buds of the tiger lily, also known as golden needles, are used mainly in Vietnam and in Chinese-style dishes in other countries. Soaked in water and drained, they add a pleasant texture and a slightly tart and tealike flavor to soups and stuffings.

Macadamia Nuts These rich, rather bland nuts are our nearest substitute for the *kemiri* or candlenut of Southeast Asia, which is unavailable here. Like candlenuts, macadamias are generally ground into sauces as a binder. Where they are called for in this book, the recipes take into account the salt that comes with the typical canned macadamias.

Mint Fresh mint gives a lift to certain Southeast Asian dishes, especially fish and poultry dishes. Spearmint or any other variety will do.

Mushrooms, Fresh The most common fresh mushroom in Southeast Asia is the straw mushroom, so called because it is cultivated in beds of rice straw. It is available here in cans from China. Our common

market mushroom is an acceptable substitute; it is similar in texture if not in flavor. Cultivated oyster mushrooms can also be used. See also Black Mushrooms.

Oils For frying and stir-frying, most Asian cooks prefer a mild or neutral-tasting vegetable oil that can stand high heat. Peanut oil, with its high smoking point and fine flavor, is the first choice, but cottonseed oil is often used for economy. Other vegetable oils such as corn, safflower, sunflower, and soybean are also suitable. The Chinese emigré cuisine of Singapore and other cities typically uses lard for stir-frying, which gives a characteristic smoky flavor to the dishes. Coconut and palm oils, though arguably authentic, are highly saturated, and most health experts advise against their use. Recipes in this book just specify oil and leave the choice up to you.

Palm Sugar A coarse brown sugar refined from palm sap, palm sugar is used throughout southern Asia for its rich, smooth flavor. It is sold in Southeast Asian and Indian markets, either as a spoonable paste or in hard blocks that must be grated. As it is relatively expensive and hard to find, none of the recipes in this book require it; but it will improve any dish calling for brown sugar.

Papaya, Green Several varieties of papaya, including not only the familiar pear-shaped variety but also some with larger football-shaped fruit, are used in Southeast Asian cooking. When the fruit is fully formed but has not begun to ripen, it is used as a vegetable, giving a mild flavor and crunchy texture to salads. Frozen green papaya from Thailand can be purchased in some Southeast Asian markets, and fresh green papayas are sometimes available from Hawaii. Do not confuse true green papayas with the green-skinned papayas often found in produce markets; the latter are partially ripe and sweeter than true green fruit. The seeds are the

indicator: In a true green papaya, they are as white as the surrounding flesh; in more mature papayas they are black.

Peanuts Although they are not native to the region, peanuts have become an integral part of almost every Southeast Asian cuisine. They may be toasted or fried and chopped for a crunchy garnish, or ground to a paste for use in sauces. Asian markets sell raw peanuts in bulk at very reasonable prices compared to the canned roasted variety. Try to get the type with the red skins attached, because the skins give a slight but pleasantly bitter edge to the flavor.

Peppercorns Before chiles were introduced from the New World, black and white pepper provided most of the "heat" in Southeast Asian cooking. They are still important spices, both to the cuisines and to the economies of the region. Black and white peppercorns come from the same tree; the latter have had the black rind removed and have a somewhat simpler, less spicy flavor. Whenever possible, use whole peppercorns and grind them just before using. Specialty spice shops often carry several varieties of both white and black pepper and at a better price than the small jars on supermarket shelves.

Rice Wine Vietnamese, Philippine, and Chinese cooking frequently use a dark-amber rice wine such as the Shaoxing variety from China. This wine is found in Chinese markets, usually labeled with the older spelling, *Shao Hsing*. Sake (Japanese rice wine) is not a particularly good substitute; instead, use a medium-bodied sherry, preferably a Spanish dry Oloroso or Amontillado.

Salam Leaves Also known as Indonesian bay leaves, these 3-inch-long dried leaves are used to flavor soups, curries, and rice dishes. Their flavor and aroma are vaguely tealike with mild fruity-spicy overtones. Salam leaves and curry leaves (see page 27) are often used interchangeably, although they are not identical.

Salt The recipes in this book were originally developed with kosher salt, a coarse, flaky, noniodized salt with a milder flavor than that of standard table salt. If you prefer to use table salt or sea salt, start with half the amount called for in the recipe and adjust to taste.

Sambal Ulek Sambal is a word with several meanings in Indonesia and Malaysia. In one sense it refers to dishes cooked with chiles, such as Sambal Cumi-Cumi (see page 96). It also covers a whole range of chile-based condiments, one of the most common of which is sambal ulek, a paste of fresh red chiles preserved with salt or vinegar. Sambal ulek is used in seasoning pastes and sauces, and can serve as a handy substitute for fresh chiles. A bottled version made by the Dutch firm Conimex (labeled with the old spelling *oelek*) is widely available. A recipe for a homemade version appears on page 37, followed by one for sambal bajak.

Shallots These small, brown-skinned onions are more authentic in Southeast Asian cooking than are our large yellow onions, but they tend to be scarce and expensive here. They are generally cheaper in Asian markets. If you can find and afford them, by all means use shallots in any pounded mixture; otherwise, use either yellow onions or the white bottoms of green onions.

Shrimp, Dried Tiny dried shrimp are a familiar sight in Asian and Latin American markets in this country. They are used in many forms throughout Southeast Asia, for both flavor and texture. They have a powerful odor when raw, but it disappears with soaking and cooking, leaving a delicious flavor. The quality and price vary widely. Choose the plumpest, pinkest dried shrimp you can find and store them in a tightly sealed jar. They will stay fresh longer if refrigerated.

Shrimp Paste (Kapi, Trasi, Blachan) This brownish, dry paste is made from fermented shrimp. If fish sauce and dried shrimp are acquired tastes, then shrimp paste is especially so, being a more concentrated form of the same flavor. However, it is as essential as coconut milk for an authentic Thai or Indonesian curry. Shrimp paste is available either dried or "fresh"—the former, a firm, mud-brown brick; the latter, a softer, pinker mixture sold in jars. The recipes in this book are written for the dried form except where noted; if you wish to substitute the fresh version, use half as much. Tightly sealed in a jar, it will keep indefinitely at room temperature.

Shrimp paste is never used raw; it is always cooked in some way. When it is to be added to a raw mixture, as in Coconut and Vegetable Salad (see page 115), wrap it in a small square of foil and heat in a dry skillet or over a charcoal fire before adding it.

Soy Sauce In Southeast Asia soy sauce is mostly identified with Chinese and Indonesian cooking. When a recipe calls for dark soy sauce, it means a Chinese-style sauce such as the Superior brand from China or the Koon Chun brand from Hong Kong. Both are darker, richer, and saltier than a typical Japanese-style sauce, such as the one made by Kikkoman. Certain Indonesian dishes call for kecap manis, a sweetened soy sauce from Java (see page 28). Otherwise, use a light Japanese-style soy.

Star Anise A spice unrelated to anise, but with a similar licorice flavor, star anise is an ingredient in the Chinese five-spice powder and is also used in Vietnamese dishes, especially with beef. It is available in Asian markets, spice shops, and some Mexican markets, where it is known as *aniz estrella*.

Sugar Unless otherwise specified, use granulated white sugar. If brown sugar is called for, use light, golden, or dark according to your taste. See also Palm Sugar.

Tamarind The seed pods of this tropical tree, which look like large fuzzy, brown bean pods, contain a tart pulp that is widely used to flavor Asian foods. Tamarind is actually more familiar to most Americans than it might seem—it is a major ingredient in Worcestershire sauce. The clean, refreshingly tart flavor of tamarind is unlike that of citrus or vinegar and goes well with the complex spice blends of Southeast Asia.

Tamarind is available in many forms, but all of them must be converted to a liquid before being added to foods. The traditional method is to break open the whole pods, soak the flesh in warm water, then pound and strain the mixture, straining out the seeds and stringy pulp. It's far easier to start with the prepared pulp sold in tightly wrapped ½-pound blocks in Asian markets (see recipe for Tamarind Water, page 34). A liquid tamarind concentrate from India, sold in plastic jars in Indian stores, is even easier to use, although finicky Southeast Asian cooks say the flavor is not as good. Just dissolve the concentrate in 6 to 7 parts warm water.

Tofu This is the Japanese name for bean curd, a highly nutritious product made from soybeans. Tofu has been made in eastern Asia for over two thousand years and is an important source of protein for millions of people. Because both Asian foods and vegetarian diets are growing in popularity in this country, tofu is becoming a common supermarket item.

Tofu is available in many forms. Regular (Japanese-style) tofu is sold packed in liquid in sealed plastic tubs. Because it is fairly fragile, it is best in soups and simmered dishes. Firm (Chinese-style) tofu comes in similar packages, but is more compressed. It holds up better in stir-fried dishes and can even be grilled. Both types are also sold in sealed foil packages that do not require refrigeration, but any leftovers must be refrigerated after opening. Triangles or blocks of fried tofu are eaten as snacks, stuffed with other ingredients, or cut up in stir-fry dishes. Dried tofu, available in sheets or sticks, can be used as a meat substitute.

Turmeric Another member of the ginger family, turmeric (*Curcuma longa*) is most familiar to Americans as the source of the yellow color in curry powder and prepared mustards. Aside from its ability to stain a sauce yellow, turmeric has a distinctively pungent flavor and aroma of its own. In Southeast Asia, it is often used fresh, minced for stir-fried dishes or pounded in a mortar with other aromatics for yellow curry pastes. Fresh turmeric is sometimes available in Asian markets; the gingerlike rhizomes have a brown skin over brilliant carrot-orange flesh. You can also find dried rhizomes and grind them to order, but only if you have a strong grinder. The ground form is much more convenient and, if relatively fresh, will do fine in any recipe in this book.

Vinegars For most Southeast Asian cooking, use a mild, pale vinegar—Japanese rice vinegar is ideal. Be sure to get the unseasoned variety; some types are flavored with salt, sugar, and MSG. Cider vinegar is an approximate substitute for rice vinegar.

Water Chestnuts Canned water chestnuts, like bamboo shoots, vary in quality from one brand to another, so it pays to try as many brands as you can find. The best ones are sweet and crunchy, with little canned flavor. Store leftovers in the same way as bamboo shoots (see page 24). Asian markets sometimes sell fresh water chestnuts. They are sweeter, crunchier, and altogether preferable to the canned variety. Look for rock-hard specimens and reject any with soft spots.

Yellow Bean Sauce This condiment of salted and preserved yellow soybeans is used as a salty ingredient in sauces in much the same way as the salted black beans of Chinese cooking. One brand from Singapore, packed in jars with liquid, is labeled Salted Soya Bean. A similar product from Hong Kong is labeled Chiu Chow Bean Sauce.

Dried ingredients (clockwise from upper right) include cloud ears, Kaffir lime leaves, dried shrimp, red chiles, black mushrooms, galangal slices, and in the center, salam leaves.

MEATS AND POULTRY

Although the quantity of meat in the Asian diet is considerably less than that in the diet of industrial countries of the West, Asian cooks are notoriously fussy about the quality of meats they use. Freshness and flavor are valued overall. Whether you buy from specialty butchers and poulterers or from a supermarket meat case, it pays to shop around and find the very best your neighborhood has to offer.

Meat-eating habits depend in large part on religious beliefs. Moslems—most Indonesians and substantial numbers in Malaysia and other countries—are forbidden to eat pork, so beef and lamb are popular. Hindus, on the other hand, do not eat beef. Southeast Asian Buddhists generally have no restrictions, although they prefer not to do the butchering themselves, leaving that task to their neighbors of other faiths. Chicken and other poultry are favored by all, except of course strict vegetarians.

Pork is the most common meat in Vietnamese, Thai, and Philippine cooking. The reason is partly economic; pigs can be raised without using scarce space for pasture, and they are an efficient way to convert table scraps and garden waste into meat. Pork also cooks quickly, conserving fuel. The more tender cuts (mainly from the loin and rib) are sliced for stir-frying or grilling; the tougher cuts are either stewed or ground to make meatballs or stuffings.

With its mild flavor, pork is equally appropriate for everything from gently seasoned stuffings to highly spiced curries. It is also surprisingly lean; in fact, well-trimmed pork is leaner than American-style beef, as the meat is not marbled with fat.

Beef (which includes the meat of both cattle and water buffalo) is a luxury meat in much of Southeast Asia, and it is used in small quantities. Cattle and buffalo are kept mainly as draft animals, since farmland is too precious to be used for pasture. The most famous beef dishes of the region, like Beef Soup With Noodles (see page 63), are from the old colonial capitals, especially in Vietnam and the Philippines, or the predominantly Moslem areas of Indonesia and Malaysia.

However, with the relative abundance of beef in this country, Southeast Asian restaurants feature many beef dishes on their menus. The best cuts of beef for stir-frying are those that balance tenderness and flavor—round, sirloin, and flatiron, a tender piece within the chuck. For stews and curries, choose the less tender but fuller-flavored cuts such as chuck, brisket, or oxtail.

Variety meats such as liver, tripe, heart, kidneys, spleen, pigs' feet, and poultry giblets are more widely used in Southeast Asian cooking than they are here. The loss is ours, as these meats offer plenty of flavor as well as varied textures.

Chicken is as popular in Southeast Asia as anywhere in the world. In fact, the familiar barnyard bird is descended from the wild jungle fowl native to that region. All parts of the chicken are savored. Breast meat is perhaps the best for saté or stir-fried dishes, but the legs, wings, backs, giblets, and even feet give their rich flavor to curries, braised dishes, and chicken stock.

Go out of your way to find a supplier of good, tasty, fresh chickens. Kosher or Chinese butchers, or those serving other ethnic markets, are likely to have the best-tasting chickens around. Unless otherwise specified, the recipes in this book are for frying chickens of about 3 to 4 pounds.

Duck is a popular meat in some parts of Southeast Asia, although ducks are often kept as much for their eggs as for their meat. Although a duck contains less meat and more fat than a chicken of similar size, the meat is tastier. Fresh ducks are available increasingly in specialty poultry shops in this country (although you might have to order them ahead of time), and most supermarkets stock or can easily get frozen ducks.

FISH AND SHELLFISH

With thousands of miles of shoreline, Southeast Asia has always looked to the sea as a major food source. Rivers, lakes, and irrigated ponds also provide an abundance of freshwater fish and shellfish. Together the products of the sea and of fresh water are a far more important source of protein in the Southeast Asian diet than are meats or poultry.

Of the types of fish found in Southeast Asia, few have exact equivalents here. However, they can be organized into a few general categories for purposes of substitution. When a recipe calls for a lean, white-fleshed fish, try one of the following: east-coast sea bass, striped bass, tilefish, or cod; gulf-coast red snapper or smaller grouper or redfish; or west-coast rockfish, also known as rock cod or Pacific snapper. Among freshwater fish, catfish, carp, bass, and pike are good choices. Some recipes call for a stronger, richer fish; good choices for these dishes include jack, mackerel, pompano, or tuna. If you want to be really authentic, some Asian markets carry frozen Southeast Asian species such as pomfret (a rich saltwater fish) and milkfish (a leaner fish, widely aquacultured in the Philippines and elsewhere).

For steaming or frying, a whole fish of 2 to 5 pounds is ideal. Fillets and steaks of larger fish can be cooked by just about any method. If possible buy seafood from a specialty market rather than in prewrapped packages. Look for a shop that does a brisk business (so the stock turns over quickly) and that does not smell too fishy; a good clean smell is a sign of a fish market that takes extra care to carry only the freshest seafood and to handle it properly. Whether you are buying whole fish, steaks, or fillets, choose those that are brightly colored and have a clean, fresh smell. For the freshest possible fish, try to buy from markets that have tanks of live catfish and other freshwater species, which can be killed and cleaned for you on the spot.

Shellfish are especially abundant in Southeast Asia. Shrimp (or prawns—the names are used somewhat interchangeably) are the most common shellfish, found in both fresh and salt water. They range in size from tiny saltwater shrimp, which are typically salted and dried or processed into shrimp paste, to an enormous freshwater prawn that may grow to be nearly as much as a foot long. U.S. cooks may use any native or Mexican shrimp or try one of several species of shrimp and prawns now being imported frozen from the Philippines, Malaysia, or other Southeast Asian countries. Crab, spiny lobster, squid, clams, and mussels are also popular, and here, too, our native species can stand in well for the Southeast Asian varieties.

Although Asian cooks generally avoid frozen fish, frozen shellfish is quite acceptable as long as it is recently thawed. Shrimp, squid, and scallops freeze particularly well. To get them at their freshest, look for those that are still frosty.

Tips

WHERE TO SHOP FOR SOUTHEAST ASIAN INGREDIENTS

Because of the growing number of Southeast Asian immigrants in the United States, many cities now have stores that sell authentic ingredients for Southeast Asian cooking. Most of these ingredients come from Thailand, Indonesia, or the Philippines, although imports from Malaysia and Singapore are increasing. Many Southeast Asian markets are located in or near Chinese communities, and larger Chinese stores often carry some Southeast Asian goods. Check the Yellow Pages under "Oriental Foods" or similar headings. Some ingredients might also be found in Indian or Middle Eastern markets.

Indonesian ingredients frequently show up in European-style delicatessens, in part because of the Dutch connection (see page 8). Conimex and Köningsvogel are two widely distributed Dutch brands of packaged Indonesian goods, including spice mixes and other condiments.

Some ingredients from Vietnam, Cambodia, and Laos are virtually unobtainable here. However, many of the ingredients typical of these cuisines (rice paper and fish sauce, for example) are manufactured in Thailand for export, often with labels in Vietnamese and Cambodian as well as in Thai, French, and English.

Philippine goods are sometimes found in Chinese markets as well as in a growing number of Filipino-owned groceries.

Once you find it, a well-stocked Asian grocery or mail-order house can supply enough exotic ingredients for a lifetime of culinary exploration. Some of the following mail-order sources offer catalogs; others respond to written requests for prices and ship on receipt of payment. For best results send a list of the desired items, including alternate names listed in the glossary. Some suppliers accept orders by telephone.

DeWildt Imports, Inc.
RD 3
Bangor, PA 18013
(215) 588-4949
A large selection of mostly Indonesian goods. Free catalog with old-style spellings; phone orders accepted.

Oriental Food Mart
909 Race Street
Philadelphia, PA 19107
(215) 922-5111
No catalog; call or write for prices.

The Oriental Market
502 Pampas Street
Austin, TX 78752
(512) 453-9058
No catalog; call or write for prices.

Vietnam House
242 Farmington Avenue
Hartford, CT 06105
(203) 524-0010
No catalog; phone orders accepted. Direct orders to Mrs. Toai.

Wing Woh Lung Co.
50 Mott Street
New York, NY 10013
(212) 962-3459
No catalog; phone orders accepted.

The following three stores specialize in Middle Eastern and/or Indian goods, but carry many Southeast Asian spices and prepared goods. Call or write for selection and prices.

Bezjian's Grocery
4725 Santa Monica Boulevard
Los Angeles, CA 90029
(213) 663-1503

Haig's Delicacies
642 Clement Street
San Francisco, CA 94118
(415) 752-6283

House of Spices
76-17 Broadway
Queens, NY 11373
(718) 476-1577

For herb plants:

Logee's Greenhouses
55 North Street
Danielson, CT 06239
(203) 774-8038

Taylor's Herb Gardens, Inc.
1535 Lone Oak Road
Vista, CA 92084
(619) 727-3485

Three basic table sauces offer variations on a single theme: top, Vietnamese Nuoc Mam Sauce; lower left, Thai Fresh Chile Sauce; and lower right, Cambodian Spicy Lime Sauce.

CONDIMENTS AND SAUCES

Although many Southeast Asian dishes are highly seasoned, the final seasoning is up to the individual diner. Whether eating in a restaurant or in a private home, you will almost always find an assortment of sauces and condiments on the table, to add whatever little touch of hot, sour, sweet, or salty flavor the food needs.

Many of the recipes in this book include recipes for specific sauces to accompany them. Recipes for other sauces with more general uses are given in this section. Some, like sambal ulek, are basic condiments used in cooking as well as at the table. Others, such as those given on opposite page under Table Sauces, are used as dipping sauces for all sorts of foods and sometimes as salad dressings. A dipping sauce can actually function as a complete dish in your menu. For example, *nam prik*, a Thai fresh chile sauce (see opposite page), is technically a sauce, and may be spooned over rice or used to

spice up other dishes; but when you order it in a Thai restaurant you get not only the sauce, but also an assortment of crunchy raw vegetables to dip in it. The Vietnamese *nuoc leo* (see page 36), which contains ground pork, rice, and chopped peanuts, is also substantial enough to blur the distinction between sauces and dishes.

KECAP MANIS

> 1 cup Japanese-style soy sauce
> ½ cup dark molasses
> 2 tablespoons brown sugar

Combine ingredients in a small saucepan over low heat. Stir to dissolve sugar. Allow to cool, then store in a jar or soy-sauce bottle.

Makes 1½ cups.

Variation Use 1⅓ cups Chinese black soy sauce (which already contains molasses), such as Koon Chun brand from Hong Kong. Omit molasses from recipe and increase sugar to ½ cup.

TAMARIND WATER

Tightly covered, Tamarind Water will keep several weeks in the refrigerator, so you might want to make a cup or more at a time. This recipe makes Tamarind Water of medium strength; some recipes specify other proportions of water to tamarind.

> 1 ounce prepared tamarind pulp (one piece about 1 by 1½ in.)
> 1 cup warm water

1. In a small bowl, cover tamarind with water and let soak until soft, about 20 minutes.

2. Break apart pulp with fingers to separate seeds and strings. Strain liquid through a fine wire strainer and discard seeds and strings. Use immediately or bottle and store in refrigerator.

Makes 1 cup.

TABLE SAUCES

One of the basic flavorings of all mainland Southeast Asian cuisines is a thin sauce of fish sauce, chile, and lime juice or vinegar. There are countless varieties, some sweeter, some hotter, some more sour. These sauces may be used for dipping fried, grilled, or steamed foods, as dressings for salads, or as condiments to be added to taste at the table. Three examples are given below, and although they are labeled by country of origin, they can be used interchangeably. In each case if you want a hotter sauce, include some of the seeds and veins of the chiles. For a milder sauce remove them.

THAI FRESH CHILE SAUCE
Nam prik
Thailand

Thai cooks make dozens of varieties of *nam prik*, which translates simply as "chile sauce." This one is on the sour end of the spectrum, with the additional accents of dried shrimp and bitter, crunchy eggplant. Tiny Thai or pea eggplants are most authentic.

> 2 tablespoons dried shrimp, soaked in water 10 minutes and drained
> 4 cloves garlic
> 2 fresh red or green chiles; stems, seeds, and veins removed; minced
> 1 teaspoon sugar
> 3 tablespoons lime juice
> 2 tablespoons fish sauce
> ¼ cup minced raw eggplant (optional)

1. *To prepare in a mortar:* Combine shrimp, garlic, and chiles and pound to a paste. Stir in sugar, lime juice, fish sauce, and eggplant (if used). *To prepare in a blender or food processor:* Combine all ingredients and blend to a smooth consistency.

2. Taste sauce for balance of hot, sweet, sour, and salty and adjust as necessary with more chiles, fish sauce, lime juice, or sugar.

Makes ½ cup.

NUOC MAM SAUCE
Nuoc cham
Vietnam

This version emphasizes the flavor of the fish sauce, so be sure to use a good one.

> 1 clove garlic
> 1 small green chile; stems, seeds, and veins removed; minced
> 3 tablespoons fish sauce
> 1 teaspoon vinegar or lime juice
> 1 teaspoon sugar
> 1 tablespoon water

To prepare in a mortar: Pound garlic and chile together, then blend in fish sauce, vinegar, sugar, and the water. *To prepare in a blender or food processor:* Combine all ingredients and blend thoroughly.

Makes ⅓ cup.

SPICY LIME SAUCE
Cambodia

Sweeter and milder than the Vietnamese or Thai table sauces, this is used as a dipping sauce and salad dressing.

> 2 cloves garlic, peeled
> 1 or 2 fresh red chiles, stems, seeds, and veins removed
> ½ cup water
> 2 tablespoons fish sauce
> Juice of 1 medium lime
> 3 tablespoons sugar
> Shredded carrot, for garnish

Combine garlic, chiles, and the water in a blender or food processor and liquify. In a small bowl, combine fish sauce, lime juice, sugar, and mixture from blender. Stir to dissolve sugar. If using sauce by itself, add a bit of shredded carrot for garnish.

Makes 1 scant cup.

FRIED ONION OR GARLIC FLAKES

Onions, shallots, or garlic, thinly sliced and fried crisp, are used to garnish many Southeast Asian dishes. Frying them to just the right consistency is tricky, however, so many cooks use commercially dehydrated flakes instead, with excellent results. Look for bags of garlic and onion flakes in Asian markets; they will be much less expensive than the ones on supermarket spice racks.

No amounts are given in the following recipe. The fried flakes keep for a few weeks in a tightly sealed jar, but it is just as easy to cook up a new batch when you need them.

> Oil
> Dehydrated onion or garlic flakes

Lightly oil a small skillet (preferably nonstick) or wok. Heat pan over medium heat until an onion or garlic flake sizzles instantly. Add flakes and cook, stirring or shaking pan, until they are lightly browned. Transfer to a plate lined with paper towels to drain and cool. Use at room temperature.

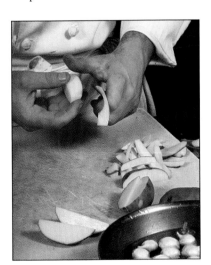

PEANUT SAUCES

Sauces based on ground peanuts are popular in Thailand, Malaysia, and Indonesia, where they invariably accompany the grilled skewered meats called saté. Thinner versions are used as a dip for vegetables, or as a salad dressing (see Gado-Gado Sauce, page 116). Any of these sauces may be made hotter or milder, sweeter or saltier, according to taste.

PEANUT SAUCE I
Indonesia

This sauce is traditionally made of peanuts ground by hand in a mortar. It can also be made in a food processor.

- *1 cup oil*
- *½ cup (2½ oz) raw peanuts*
- *2 tablespoons minced shallot*
- *1 tablespoon minced garlic*
- *1 teaspoon ground dried chile or ½ teaspoon sambal ulek*
- *¼ to ½ cup thin coconut milk (see page 38)*
- *1 tablespoon lime juice*
- *1 tablespoon kecap manis*
- *½ teaspoon brown or palm sugar, or to taste*

1. Heat oil in a wok over high heat until a peanut sizzles instantly when added to oil. Add peanuts and fry until they begin to brown; turn off heat. Transfer peanuts with a slotted spoon or Chinese skimmer to mortar, blender, or food processor.

2. *To prepare in a mortar:* Pound to a slightly gritty paste. Remove peanut paste from mortar and set aside. Add shallot, garlic, and chile to mortar and pound to a coarse paste. *To prepare in a blender or food processor:* Add ¼ cup coconut milk and process to a paste, scraping bowl often. Mince shallot, garlic, and chile together as finely as possible.

3. Remove all but 1 tablespoon oil from pan and reserve for another use. Reheat oil over medium heat, add shallot mixture, and cook until fragrant but not browned. Add peanut paste, ¼ cup of the coconut milk, lime juice, and kecap manis. Cook, stirring and scraping pan to prevent scorching, until thoroughly blended and fairly thick. Add sugar to taste. If sauce is too thick, thin with additional coconut milk.

Makes about ¾ cup.

PEANUT SAUCE II
Thailand

With Tamarind Water and curry paste on hand in the refrigerator, this sauce can be whipped up in only a few minutes.

- *¼ cup coconut cream (see page 38)*
- *1 tablespoon Red Curry Paste I or II (see page 75)*
- *3 tablespoons crunchy peanut butter*
- *1 tablespoon Tamarind Water (see page 34) or lime juice*
- *¼ to ½ cup thin coconut milk*
- *1½ teaspoons brown or palm sugar*
- *Fish sauce, to taste*

In a small pan heat coconut cream and curry paste over medium heat until bubbly. Add peanut butter, Tamarind Water, ¼ cup coconut milk, and sugar; cook, stirring and scraping pan to prevent scorching, until sauce is reduced to a smooth consistency. Season to taste with fish sauce and thin if necessary with additional coconut milk.

Makes about ½ cup.

NUOC LEO I
Vietnam

This soybean and rice sauce is traditionally served with Pork-Filled Crêpe-Omelets (see page 50) and with simmered or grilled beef dishes. It is also good as a dip for raw vegetables.

- *2 tablespoons glutinous rice*
- *¾ cup water*
- *1 tablespoon oil*
- *2 cloves garlic, minced*
- *2 ounces ground pork*
- *2 tablespoons yellow bean sauce, mashed, or Chinese ground bean sauce*
- *1 cup water or Basic Chicken Stock (see page 62)*
- *1 teaspoon sugar*
- *¼ cup peanuts, toasted and ground*

1. Bring rice and the ¾ cup water to a boil, reduce heat, cover, and simmer until water is absorbed and rice is quite soft.

2. In a small skillet heat oil over medium-low heat and cook garlic until fragrant. Add pork and cook until it loses its raw color. Add bean sauce, rice, the 1 cup water, and sugar and simmer until quite thick. Stir in peanuts and serve warm or at room temperature.

Makes 1½ cups.

NUOC LEO II

This version uses *tuong*, a sweet and salty Vietnamese sauce made of soybeans and glutinous rice. It is available in well-stocked Asian markets.

- *1 tablespoon oil*
- *2 cloves garlic, minced*
- *2 ounces ground pork*
- *1 cup water or Basic Chicken Stock (see page 62)*
- *¼ cup tuong*
- *¼ cup peanuts, toasted and ground*

In a small skillet heat oil over medium-low heat and cook garlic until fragrant. Add pork and cook until it loses its raw color. Add the water and tuong and simmer until thickened. Stir in peanuts and serve warm or at room temperature.

Makes 1 cup.

SAMBAL ULEK
Fresh red-chile paste
Indonesia and Malaysia

Fresh red chiles are often hard to find; when you can find them, it pays to buy extra and preserve them as a paste. Sambal Ulek is traditionally made in a mortar, but a food processor or blender is a real timesaver.

- ¼ pound fresh red chiles, stems removed
- 1 teaspoon kosher salt
- 1 teaspoon mild vinegar (optional)

In a blender or food processor, chop chiles to a coarse paste; add salt partway through blending. Transfer to a jar and store covered in refrigerator. Will keep up to 2 weeks; for longer storage, add vinegar.

SAMBAL BAJAK
Fried red-pepper sauce
Indonesia

This popular sambal is as common in Indonesia as *nuoc cham* is in Vietnam or *nam prik* in Thailand. It is typically added to rice or stirred into soups. It packs quite a punch, so use it sparingly at first.

- 8 macadamia nuts
- ¼ pound fresh red chiles, stems removed
- 1 medium onion, peeled and quartered
- 4 cloves garlic, peeled
- ½ teaspoon shrimp paste
- 1 tablespoon brown or palm sugar
- 2 tablespoons oil
- 1 salam leaf or curry leaf (optional)
- ¼ cup water

1. *To prepare in a mortar:* Pound nuts to a coarse paste. Mince chiles, onion, and garlic and add to mortar with shrimp paste and sugar. Pound

mixture to a coarse paste. *To prepare in a food processor:* Combine macadamia nuts, chiles, onion, garlic, shrimp paste, and sugar, and process to a coarse paste. Add 1 or 2 tablespoons of water if necessary to facilitate blending.

2. In a small skillet or saucepan, heat oil over medium heat. Add chile paste and salam leaf and cook, stirring, until fragrant. Add the water and continue cooking until water has evaporated and oil begins to separate. Serve warm or at room temperature, or store in a tightly covered jar in a cool place.

Makes 1 cup.

Fresh red chiles are the base for two popular Indonesian condiments. Freshly minced and combined with salt and vinegar, they make Sambal Ulek, at right; combined with onions, garlic, and nuts and then fried, they become Sambal Bajak.

COCONUTS AND COCONUT MILK

The coconut is as essential in Southeast Asian cooking as are dairy products in northern Europe or the olive and its oil in southern Europe. Although the meat, juice, and oil all have their uses, the most common form in which coconut is used is coconut milk.

Coconut milk is not the same thing as the juice that is found inside the nut; the latter is drunk as a refreshing liquid and is used only occasionally in cooking. The milk is a rich, creamy liquid extract made from the grated meat of mature coconuts (the type at right in photograph, opposite).

In a traditional Southeast Asian kitchen, making coconut milk is a daily chore, but Western cooks have it a little easier. Canned coconut milk is an excellent and convenient product. Most comes from Thailand, Malaysia, or the Philippines; brands vary in quality, so find one you like and stick with it. Occasionally, the liquid may show a brownish or gray discoloration on top, in which case it should be discarded. If the canned variety is not available in your area, you can make coconut milk yourself from either grated fresh coconut or dried unsweetened coconut flakes (see recipe, at right).

Like dairy milk, coconut milk varies in fat content, canned versions generally being richer than homemade. Various forms are not entirely interchangeable, so the recipes in this book specify either "thick," "medium," or "thin" coconut milk. For thick coconut milk use the canned version, shaking it before opening to "homogenize" the milk, or prepare the recipe on this page with whole milk. For medium coconut milk, dilute the canned version with half its volume of water, or skim off most of the cream, or prepare the homemade with water. For thin coconut

milk, dilute canned milk with an equal volume of water or make a second extraction of the homemade.

Some recipes call for coconut cream, the concentrated, oil-rich portion of the coconut milk that rises to the top, like cream on unhomogenized milk. A thick layer of cream usually clings to the lid of a can of coconut milk. Some cream also rises to the top of homemade coconut milk, especially when it is refrigerated. Coconut cream can be used in place of oil to cook curry pastes and to facilitate mixing ingredients when using a blender.

If a recipe calls for coconut cream to be used separately, be careful not to shake the can before opening it.

To open a fresh coconut, hold it in one hand with the three "eyes" uppermost. Strike the shell an inch or two away from the eyes with a hammer or the back edge of a heavy cleaver. After several blows, the shell will begin to crack and the liquid will seep out. Smell and taste the liquid—if it is sour or rancid, the coconut is spoiled and should be discarded.

Another method of cracking a coconut is to bake it in a 400° F oven for 15 minutes, by which time the shell will usually split. If it has not done so, it should at least be easier to crack with a hammer or cleaver. Do not bake longer, however, or the flesh will begin to cook.

Once a large crack has appeared, use a clean screwdriver or an oyster knife (but not a kitchen knife) to pry the shell open, and pry the white meat away from the shell. There is no need to remove the brown skin. The meat is now ready to be grated with a box grater (see photograph, opposite) or the grating disk of a food processor. The traditional tool for grating coconut, a spoon-shaped piece of metal with a sawtooth edge, is shown in photograph, opposite.

The traditional way to extract coconut milk is to squeeze the grated and soaked meat in a bundle of the fibers from the coconut shell. In a modern kitchen, a fine strainer will do the job. For a more thorough extraction, wrap the grated coconut in a clean, strong towel or a piece of

clean nylon stocking and twist to wring out every last drop of liquid.

After the milk has been extracted, the coconut gratings will have little flavor or nutritive value left and should be discarded. In Southeast Asia, they go to the chickens.

COCONUT MILK

Homemade coconut milk can be made from fresh, frozen, or dried coconut. Frozen grated coconut from the Philippines is available in some Asian markets. If using dried coconut, be sure to get the unsweetened variety, sold mainly in health-food stores. In Southeast Asia, coconut milk is usually made with water. Western cooks may also use cow's milk, which gives a richer extract. If using milk, be careful to avoid scorching the milk during the boiling step.

2 cups water or milk
2 cups grated unsweetened coconut flakes or shreds

1. Bring water to a boil in a saucepan. Add coconut, remove from heat, and let cool to room temperature.

2. Transfer mixture to a food processor or blender. Blend 1 minute at high speed.

3. Strain mixture through a fine wire strainer, pressing hard with a wooden spoon to extract as much liquid as possible. Use immediately or refrigerate covered up to 3 days.

4. If desired, make a second extraction from the same coconut by repeating steps 1 through 3. This will make a thinner milk.

Makes 2 cups thick coconut milk (plus optional 2 cups thin coconut milk).

<u>Note</u> The oils in coconut milk become rancid quickly at room temperature. It will keep for a day or two in the refrigerator, but for longer storage, freeze it in plastic storage containers or in locking food-storage bags. However, frozen coconut milk never has quite the smooth texture of the fresh or canned version.

Frying, in all its forms, is especially popular for fish and shellfish. Chiles often figure prominently in these dishes.

Deep-Frying, Pan-Frying & Stir-Frying

When done right, cooking
in oil—deep-frying, pan-frying,
and stir-frying—produces excellent
results, crisp and flavorful but never greasy.
Southeast Asian cooks use these techniques
to turn out all sorts of delicious dishes, from
crisp-fried meatballs wrapped in
noodles (see page 47) to delicate stir-fried
vegetables (see the Vietnamese Family
Supper menu, page 56) and an unusual
combination crêpe and omelet (see page 50).
With the tips in this chapter,
you, too, can turn out delicious Southeast
Asian deep-fried, pan-fried,
and stir-fried dishes with a minimum
of added calories.

COOKING WITH OIL

Although they may sound quite similar, stir-frying, pan-frying, and deep-frying are actually three distinct cooking techniques involving different amounts of oil. Stir-frying uses the least oil; the ingredients are quickly cooked in just enough oil to keep them from sticking to the pan. Pan-frying, or sautéing, uses a more generous amount of oil, which may or may not be part of the finished dish. Deep-fried foods, as the name implies, are cooked in an ample amount of oil, then drained before serving.

DEEP-FRYING

Frying, also called deep-frying, is an important technique in Southeast Asian cooking. In a sense, "deep-frying" is redundant, because without any qualifying label "frying" means cooking foods by immersing them in hot oil. In true frying, the food is cooked only by the heat of the oil, not from direct contact with the pan.

The bad name that fried foods have received in recent years is not entirely deserved. Badly fried foods can absorb a lot of oil, making them both unhealthful and unappetizing; but with good technique, you can fry foods with a minimum of oil absorption. And there's nothing like frying for cooking foods quickly and producing a crunchy exterior.

There's no mystery to good frying in any cuisine, East or West. The critical factors are the quality of the oil, its temperature, and the coating on the foods to be fried.

The best oil for frying is a clear, relatively flavorless vegetable oil with a high smoking point (an ability to withstand high temperatures without burning). Peanut oil is the choice of most Asian cooks. It is relatively expensive, but unlike some cheaper oils, it can be reused several times. Corn oil is a close second to peanut in performance, and it's quite a bit less expensive. Cottonseed oil is one of the least expensive, but it is less durable than peanut or corn oil.

Oil temperature is critical. For best results, the oil should be between 360 and 390° F. At this temperature, the batter or other coating seals almost instantly, preventing any further absorption of oil. Too-hot oil can burn the outside of the food before the inside is fully cooked. The oil itself will begin to burn at over 400° F, giving a burnt flavor to the food. Too-cool oil is equally bad; below 350° F, the food will absorb a lot of oil before it is cooked.

To control oil temperature, either fry in a thermostatically controlled deep-fryer or use a thermometer specially made for deep-frying and candy-making. Whether the thermometer is of the straight-line or dial type, it should be easy to read, have a range of up to at least 400° F, and have a clip or other way to attach it to the pan. Look for a thermometer with a stem long enough to sink 2 inches or more into the oil. Accuracy is important. To test a new thermometer, place it in a pot of boiling water. At sea level it should read exactly 212° F, and at higher altitudes approximately 2° F less per 1,000 feet of elevation. If it is off by more than a few degrees, return it and look for another.

To keep the temperature up during frying, do not fry too many pieces of food at a time. Watch the temperature; if it drops below 350° F and does not recover quickly, you are frying too much food for the quantity of oil. One solution is to use as much oil as you safely and conveniently can. Be careful, however, to leave enough room for the oil to bubble up during frying. As a general rule, the frying container should be no more than two-thirds full of oil.

Frying presents certain dangers, particularly burns and oil fires. To avoid being burned by splattering oil, be sure that all the foods to be fried are as dry as possible. Gently lower foods into hot oil rather than dropping them from a height. Some splattering is inevitable, however, so wear long sleeves or long oven mitts. Shielding yourself with a wok cover when adding foods also helps. However, do not cover the wok while frying; the steam released by the

frying foods can condense on the cover and drip back into the oil when you lift the cover, creating even more splattering.

To prevent oil spills and possible fires, never fill the pan more than two-thirds full, and be sure the pan is stable. Never use a round-bottomed wok for frying without its supporting ring, and the ring is recommended with a flat-bottomed wok as well. Never leave a pan full of hot oil unattended.

FISH CAKES
Tod mun
Thailand

The not-quite-crisp outside and vaguely chewy inside texture of these tasty morsels may seem odd at first, but by the second or third bite most people are hooked. And after the fish cakes are gone, you will probably look for something else to dip into the tangy cucumber sauce.

½ pound fillet of lean white fish
1 tablespoon red curry paste
1 teaspoon fish sauce
¼ cup green beans, sliced diagonally as thinly as possible
Oil, for deep-frying
Fresh coriander, for garnish

Cucumber Sauce

¼ cup sugar
¼ teaspoon kosher salt
¼ cup rice vinegar or distilled vinegar
¼ cup peeled and diced cucumber
1 small fresh chile, thinly sliced

In a food processor or meat grinder, grind fish as finely as possible. Transfer to a bowl and mix in curry paste, fish sauce, and green beans. Form into 2-inch round cakes ½ inch thick. Heat oil to 375° F and fry until golden brown. Garnish with coriander leaves, and serve with dipping bowls of Cucumber Sauce.

Serves 4 to 6 with other dishes.

Cucumber Sauce In a small bowl, dissolve sugar and salt in vinegar. Add cucumber and chile and let stand a few minutes before serving.

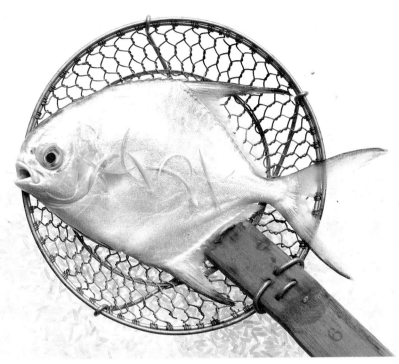

Basics

DEEP-FRYING TECHNIQUES

The following basic steps apply to deep-frying anything from a dozen lumpia to a whole fish in a wok.

□ *Organize.* Give yourself plenty of room to work, and have ready all the hand tools you need—a standard-sized wire skimmer for retrieving, paper towels for draining, serving dishes, and perhaps a wok cover to shield against splatters. Another useful tool is a fine-mesh wire skimmer for removing bits of batter from the oil before they burn. If food to be fried needs to be marinated or a batter needs time to rest after mixing, the time to do it is while you are organizing your equipment. If you will be holding foods before serving, heat the oven to low.

□ *Heat oil.* Set up the wok or other frying pan. Be sure to use the wok ring for stability, even with a flat-bottomed wok, and position the handles where they won't be acci-

dentally bumped. Clip the thermometer on the side of the pan in a position where you can read it easily. Add oil to no more than two thirds the capacity of the pan. Turn the heat to high, bring the oil to the desired temperature, and reduce the heat to low.

□ *Coat.* Except for the fritters on page 122, the recipes for fried dishes in this book don't use complicated batters. Many Southeast Asian fried foods have only a light dusting of cornstarch, or no coating at all.

□ *Fry.* If you are frying many small items, start with one or two pieces. Watch the temperature; it will drop slightly, but should return to the desired temperature within 30 seconds. If not, turn the heat back to high, let the oil return to cooking temperature, and try again. Adjust the heat and the number of items fried so that the oil never drops below 350° F for more than a few seconds.

□ *Drain.* Retrieve cooked foods from the oil with the wire skimmer. Hold the skimmer over the oil for a few seconds to drain, then transfer the

food to a plate or tray lined with paper towels to drain further. If you are frying many items, transfer the cooked pieces to a low oven to keep warm. Some wok sets come with a curved wire draining rack that clips over the side of the wok, over the hot oil. These racks are handy, as long as they don't interfere with your ability to reach all the frying foods.

□ *Clean up and save oil.* Wiping up the area around the wok right after frying is easier than cleaning up cold oil later. Most frying oils can be used at least two or three times, often more, if carefully strained and stored after each use. When the oil has cooled enough to be handled safely, ladle or pour it through a filter of several layers of cheesecloth (coffee filters are more thorough, but very slow) into a clean storage container. Seal tightly and store away from heat. Oil can be reused until it has become noticeably dark or has a strong cooked smell. Most cooks prefer to keep oil used for frying fish separate and reuse it only for fish.

SINGAPORE'S NONYA CUISINE

If all of Southeast Asia is a crossroads, then the island city-state of Singapore is its intersection, where the Straits of Singapore and Malacca link the South China Sea to the Indian Ocean. Lying just off the tip of the Malay Peninsula, Singapore is a largely Chinese city with Malay and Indian minorities.

When the British first brought large numbers of Chinese workers to Malaya, they were virtually all men. Some of them married Malay women, giving rise to a mixed population whose culture and, above all, food habits combined Chinese and Malay elements. Women of this mixed heritage are known as Nonyas, and the hybrid cooking style of Singapore and certain cities of Malaysia is known as Straits Chinese or Nonya cuisine.

Although many of the foods in Nonya cooking are typically Chinese (pork and fermented soybeans, for example), they are often combined with such non-Chinese ingredients as fermented shrimp paste and coconut milk. Many dishes begin with a Malay-style *rempah*, a mixture of spices, onion, and garlic ground together in a mortar. The rempah is slowly cooked in oil as a first step, as opposed to the rapid stir-frying typical of Chinese cooking.

FRIED WHOLE FISH, NONYA STYLE
Ikan goreng tauceo
Singapore

The Nonya cooking of Malaysia and Singapore blends Chinese and Malay traditions (see Special Note, left). The salted soybeans in this sauce show a Chinese influence, but the other ingredients—shrimp paste, galangal, lemongrass, and chile—are typically Southeast Asian.

> 1 whole (about 1½ lb) snapper, rockfish, porgy, or similar fish
> Salt
> 1 medium onion or ¼ pound shallots, chopped
> 2 cloves garlic, chopped
> 1 stalk lemongrass, thinly sliced
> ½ teaspoon shrimp paste (optional)
> 3 fresh red or green chiles, seeds and veins removed, chopped, or ½ teaspoon chile powder
> 2 slices fresh galangal or 1 teaspoon ground
> ⅓ cup (approximately) cornstarch
> Oil, for deep-frying
> 2 tablespoons yellow bean sauce, mashed
> ⅓ cup Tamarind Water (see page 34)
> Pinch sugar
> Fresh coriander or basil, for garnish (optional)

1. Prepare fish as directed on page 19. Pat dry with paper towels, sprinkle lightly with salt, and set aside.

2. In a mortar, food processor, or blender, combine onion, garlic, lemongrass, shrimp paste (if used), chiles, and galangal and process to a paste.

3. Pat fish dry again and dust liberally with cornstarch, rubbing it into cuts in sides.

4. Fill a wok or deep skillet with oil to a depth of at least 2 inches (allow room for oil to rise when fish is added). Heat oil to 375° F. Carefully add fish to oil, placing it on its side. Ladle oil over any exposed part of fish. Fry fish on both sides, turning once with slotted spoons or Chinese wire skimmer, until a skewer easily penetrates thickest part. Lift fish out of oil and let drain over pan, then transfer to warm serving platter.

5. Turn off heat under frying oil, allow to cool, and reserve for frying fish another time. In another skillet or wok, heat 2 tablespoons oil over medium heat (some of the frying oil can be used for this step). Add seasoning paste and cook, stirring, until quite fragrant. Add yellow bean sauce, cook another few seconds, and add Tamarind Water and sugar. Cook sauce until slightly thickened.

6. Blot away any accumulated oil from fish platter and pour sauce over fish. Garnish with sprigs of coriander, if desired.

Serves 4 with other dishes.

FRIED TOFU

Deep-fried tofu is used everywhere in Southeast Asia as a hot appetizer with a dipping sauce (see page 35) or as a meat substitute. The first step of pressing the tofu may not be necessary if your tofu is firm enough; just drain it thoroughly. Most Japanese-style tofu will have to be pressed.

> 1 package (7 oz) firm Chinese-style tofu
> Oil, for deep-frying

1. Drain tofu cakes well. Wrap in a clean kitchen towel or several thicknesses of paper towel, place in a plate set on a sheet pan, and invert another plate on top. Place a 1-pound weight (canned food, a cookbook, etc.) on the top plate. Let stand 30 minutes, unwrap, and drain. The tofu will have exuded a lot of liquid. The recipe may be prepared ahead of time to this point and refrigerated.

2. Slice pressed tofu into squares, triangles, or other shapes about ⅜ inch thick. Heat oil to 350° F in a wok or other deep pan. Fry tofu pieces a few at a time until puffy and golden brown, 6 to 8 minutes.

Serves 4 to 6 as an appetizer.

FRIED COCONUT CHICKEN
Ayam goreng kalasan
Indonesia

This tender, aromatic chicken is first simmered in seasoned coconut milk, then fried to produce a crisp brown skin. The technique is native to Java, as is this mildly flavored dish; Sumatran cooks make a hotter chile-flavored version.

> 1 stalk lemongrass
> 1 tablespoon minced fresh turmeric or ½ teaspoon dried
> 1 tablespoon minced fresh galangal or 1 teaspoon dried
> 1 medium onion, diced
> 2 cups medium coconut milk (see page 38)
> 3 tablespoons coconut cream, skimmed from the medium coconut milk
> 2 Kaffir lime leaves
> 3 or 4 sprigs fresh coriander, plus leaves for garnish
> Salt, to taste
> 1 small frying chicken, disjointed, or 2 to 3 pounds chicken parts
> Oil, for deep-frying

1. Thinly slice the bottom third of the lemongrass; cut tops into 2-inch sections and set aside. *To prepare in a mortar:* Combine sliced lemongrass, turmeric, galangal, and onion and pound to a smooth paste. *To prepare in a blender:* Add 2 tablespoons coconut cream to facilitate blending.

2. Spoon 3 tablespoons coconut cream (or 1 tablespoon if cream was used in step 1) into a wok or large saucepan set over medium-high heat. Add paste and cook, stirring, until thick and fragrant. Add coconut milk, lime leaves, coriander, lemongrass tops, and salt and bring to a boil. Add chicken pieces and simmer until tender (about 30 to 40 minutes).

3. When chicken is done, remove from sauce and drain thoroughly. Bring sauce to a boil and reduce by half.

4. Heat oil in another wok or frying pan to 375° F. Fry chicken pieces until crisp. (The sugar in the coconut milk will brown quickly to a mahogany color.) Transfer to serving platter, spoon sauce over chicken, and garnish with coriander leaves.

Serves 4 with other dishes.

Fried Whole Fish, Nonya Style, typifies the Straits Chinese cooking style of Singapore and Malaysia. A pounded mixture of lemongrass, chiles, and shrimp paste gives an unmistakably Southeast Asian flavor to the Chinese-style bean sauce.

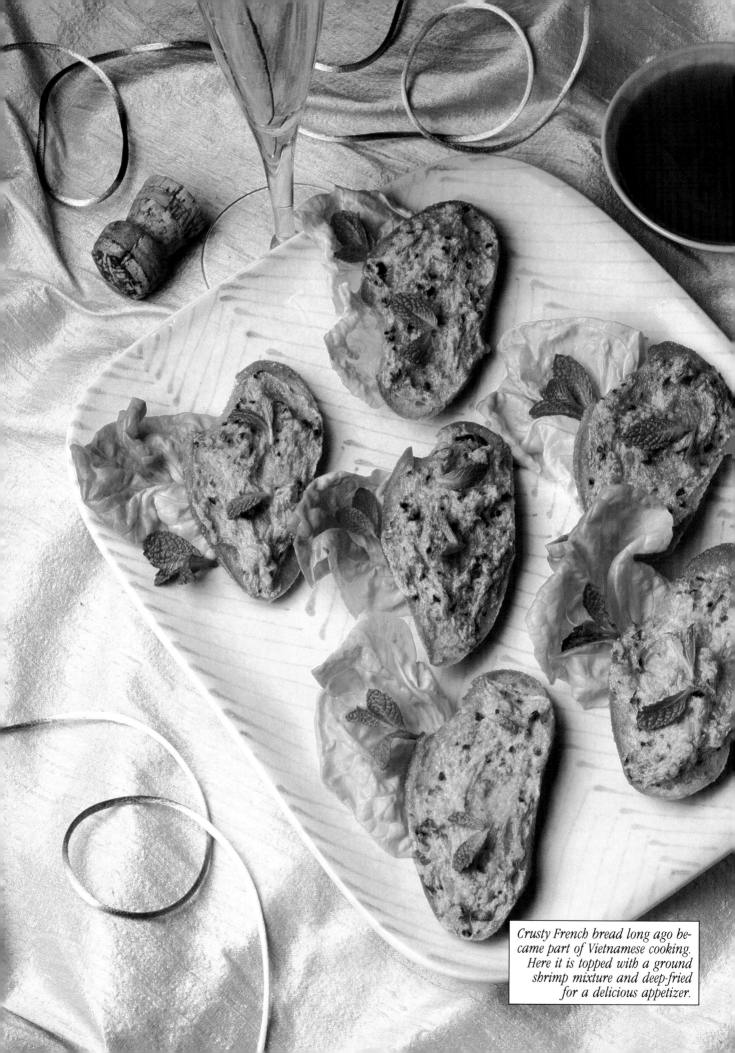

Crusty French bread long ago became part of Vietnamese cooking. Here it is topped with a ground shrimp mixture and deep-fried for a delicious appetizer.

SHRIMP TOAST
Vietnam

The use of French bread in this dish suggests that it originated during the French colonial period. It has since spread to China and other countries. In view of its East-West heritage, it would be quite appropriate to serve at a Western-style cocktail party.

> 1 baguette or small French loaf, preferably day old
> Fresh Shrimp Paste
> Oil, for deep-frying
> Butter lettuce or other tender lettuce leaves
> Mint or coriander leaves
> Nuoc Mam Sauce (see page 35)

Fresh Shrimp Paste

> ½ pound raw shrimp, peeled and deveined
> 1 tablespoon minced fresh pork fat
> 1 green onion, chopped
> 1 teaspoon fish sauce
> ¼ teaspoon kosher salt
> Pinch white or freshly ground black pepper

1. Slice bread (diagonally if using baguettes, straight across if using larger loaves) about ½ inch thick. If using day-old bread, spread slices out on a tray to dry while preparing Fresh Shrimp Paste; if using fresh bread, toast in a low oven until dried out, about 10 minutes.

2. Spread Fresh Shrimp Paste in an even ¼-inch layer on one side of bread slices. Smooth the surface with a knife dipped in cold water.

3. Fill a wok or skillet with oil to a depth of at least 1 inch. Heat oil to 350° F, then reduce heat to low. Add one or two shrimp toasts, shrimp side down, and fry until golden brown, about 1 minute. Turn and cook 45 seconds to 1 minute on other side. Lift out of oil with a slotted spoon or wire skimmer, drain over oil, then transfer to paper towels to drain further. Continue frying toasts a few at a time. Adjust heat if necessary to maintain oil temperature.

4. Serve with lettuce leaves for wrapping toasts, mint or coriander leaves

to tuck inside, and Nuoc Mam Sauce for dipping.

Makes 18 toasts; serves 4 with other dishes.

Fresh Shrimp Paste *To prepare in a blender or food processor:* Combine shrimp, pork fat, and green onion and chop to a smooth, fluffy paste. *To prepare in a mortar:* Mince together shrimp, pork fat, and green onion and pound to a smooth, fluffy texture. Add fish sauce, salt, and pepper and blend thoroughly. May be made up to a day ahead and stored covered in the refrigerator.

MEATBALLS WRAPPED IN NOODLES
Moo sarong
Thailand

This delightful appetizer presents tender minced pork in a crunchy wrapper of fried noodles, with a salty nugget of preserved egg in the center. It goes equally well with a Thai meal or a Western-style cocktail.

> 1 pound ground or minced pork
> 1 tablespoon each *minced coriander root and garlic*
> 1 teaspoon each *kosher salt and freshly ground pepper*
> 1 uncooked egg
> 1 tablespoon flour
> 1 cup finely chopped water chestnuts, bamboo shoots, or black mushrooms, or a combination
> Yolk of 1 hard-cooked egg (see Note)
> ½ pound fresh or dried thin egg noodles
> Oil, for deep-frying
> Butter lettuce or other tender lettuce leaves (optional)
> Soy sauce
> Liquid chile sauce

1. Combine pork, coriander root, garlic, salt, pepper, egg, flour, and chopped vegetables and blend thoroughly. If using a food processor, chop vegetables and seasonings together first, then add pork and egg and grind to a smooth paste.

2. Form meat mixture into 1-inch balls, embedding a small piece of cooked egg yolk in the center of each.

3. If using dried noodles, soak in warm water just long enough to soften; drain. Wrap each meatball in a few strands of noodle, enclosing ball completely.

4. Bring oil in frying pan to 360° F and fry balls a few at a time until golden brown. Cut one open after frying to be sure meat is thoroughly cooked; if not, reduce oil temperature and increase cooking time. Serve as is or wrapped in lettuce leaves, with soy sauce seasoned to taste and chile sauce for dipping.

Makes 36 meatballs; serves 6 to 8 with other dishes.

Note Use either regular hard-cooked eggs or, to be authentic, try the bright orange yolk of salted duck eggs. Look for the type labeled salted eggs. Unlike other preserved eggs, the salted variety needs to be cooked.

SHRIMP CHIPS
Krupuk or *Banh phong tom*
Indonesia and Vietnam

Like potato chips, these crisp crackers made of shrimp and tapioca starch are irresistible. The uncooked chips are sold in cellophane-wrapped boxes with multilingual labels. Straight from the package, they are inedible, but when fried they swell to more than twice their size in a few seconds. Vietnamese versions are often brightly colored.

> Oil, for deep-frying
> Dried shrimp chips (see Note)

In a wok or deep skillet, heat oil to 360° F. Fry chips a few at a time; if oil is at the proper temperature they will begin to swell in 2 to 3 seconds. Fry until lightly colored, about 15 seconds—turning is not necessary. Drain on paper towels. Chips may be fried several hours to several days ahead of time, allowed to cool, and stored in a sealed container.

Note Shrimp chips must be completely dry to fry properly, so keep the box tightly sealed. If they become soft, dry them in a low oven for 10 to 15 minutes before frying.

PAN-FRYING

Many Southeast Asian dishes commonly called fried fall between the extremes of deep-frying (cooking in ample oil) and stir-frying (cooking in the bare minimum of oil). These dishes can be grouped under the general term *pan-frying*, which corresponds to Western-style sautéing.

Unlike deep-fried foods, pan-fried foods get their heat both from the oil and from the surface of the pan. Compared to stir-frying, the pieces of food are often larger, and they cook more slowly. As in stir-frying, some or all of the cooking oil is typically included as part of the final sauce. The sauce ingredients may be cooked along with the meat or fish, or the sauce may be prepared separately.

No special equipment is required for pan-frying. Either a wok or a heavy skillet will do, as will a typical Western assortment of spatulas and tongs. Paper towels are handy for wiping excess oil out of a pan before beginning the sauce.

As in deep-frying, temperature is important. If the pan and oil are not hot enough, the food will absorb too much oil and be greasy. On the other hand, it is easy to scorch foods in a too-hot pan, as the smaller amount of oil cannot moderate the temperature the way a larger quantity can. If the oil begins to smoke, the temperature is too high.

In Southeast Asia, pan-frying is popular for seafood. One technique is known in Indonesia and Malaysia as *sambal goreng*, which may be translated as "chile-fried." Besides providing the cooking medium, the oil in a sambal goreng has the essential role of carrying the flavor of the chiles and other seasonings.

GREEN BEAN AND DRIED SHRIMP SAMBAL
Sambal goreng buncis udang kering
Indonesia and Malaysia

Like many dishes labeled sambal, these chile-spiked beans go a long way. If you prefer them as a vegetable rather than as a condiment, add more beans or decrease the chile.

2 tablespoons dried shrimp
¼ cup chopped shallot or yellow onion
2 cloves garlic, chopped
1 or 2 red chiles with seeds, minced, or ½ teaspoon sambal ulek
½ teaspoon kosher salt
2 tablespoons oil
½ pound green beans or Chinese long beans, thinly sliced on the diagonal

1. In a bowl cover dried shrimp with water and soak 15 minutes; drain.

2. In a mortar, food processor, or blender, pound together shallot, garlic, chile, and salt to a paste. Add some of the oil if necessary to facilitate blending by machine.

3. In a wok or skillet, heat oil and paste over medium-low heat until quite fragrant and oil is stained red. Turn heat to medium-high and add green beans and drained shrimp. Cook, stirring, until beans are done but still crunchy. Serve warm or at room temperature.

Serves 4 to 6 with other dishes.

FRIED FISH STEAKS IN COCONUT MILK
Sambal goreng ikan
Malaysia

This dish is relatively mild, as *sambal goreng* dishes go. The ideal fish for this treatment is one that can be cut crosswise into rather small steaks—mullet, sablefish, mackerel, or small lingcod.

1 cup chopped onion
2 cloves garlic, chopped
2 fresh chiles or ½ teaspoon sambal ulek
1 stalk lemongrass, thinly sliced
4 macadamia nuts
Pinch salt
½ teaspoon shrimp paste
3 tablespoons oil
1 pound fish steaks, about 1 inch thick
Juice of 1 lime or lemon
¾ cup thick coconut milk (see page 38)
Coconut cream, skimmed from the thick coconut milk (optional)

1. In a mortar, food processor, or blender, combine onion, garlic, chile, lemongrass, macadamia nuts, salt, and shrimp paste and process to a smooth paste. Add a little coconut cream if necessary to facilitate blending. Set aside.

2. In a skillet or wok, heat oil over medium-high heat and fry fish steaks until just barely done, 3 to 5 minutes on each side. Remove fish and set aside. Swab out about half the oil with a paper towel. Add paste and cook, stirring, until strong fragrance dissipates. Add lime juice and coconut milk and reduce by half. Return fish steaks to sauce and continue cooking until oil begins to separate. Serve fish topped with sauce.

Serves 4 with other dishes.

PAN-FRIED FISH WITH GINGER-MUSHROOM SAUCE
Cambodia

This brightly colored and flavored sauce goes equally well on fried or steamed fish; for a steamed version, see page 68. Use an assortment of mushrooms for a variety of flavors and textures. This recipe makes enough sauce for one good-sized fish or several smaller ones.

1½ to 2 pounds whole or pan-dressed fish—catfish, snapper, perch, or smaller sea bass or rockfish, prepared as directed on page 19
¼ cup Tamarind Water (see page 34)
1 teaspoon sugar
½ cup Basic Chicken Stock (see page 62)
Dash black soy sauce or kecap manis
2 tablespoons oil
1 tablespoon dried garlic flakes
2 tablespoons finely shredded fresh ginger
1 teaspoon yellow bean sauce
¼ cup assorted sliced mushrooms
1 tablespoon dried shrimp
1 green onion, cut into 2-inch lengths
¼ cup sliced yellow onion

1 ounce bean threads, soaked
  until soft and drained
  (optional)
½ cup oil
  Cornstarch
  Fresh coriander, for garnish

1. If using whole fish, have it cleaned and scaled; head may be left on or removed, as you like.

2. In a small saucepan, combine Tamarind Water and sugar and bring to a boil. Reduce to 2 tablespoons, remove from heat, and add stock and soy sauce.

3. Heat oil in a skillet over low heat. Fry garlic flakes and set aside. Turn heat to medium-high, add ginger and yellow bean sauce, and cook until fragrant. Add mushrooms, dried shrimp, and green and yellow onion and cook until vegetables soften. Add stock mixture and bean threads, if used; bring to a boil. Reduce by half, taste for seasoning, and keep warm.

4. In another skillet or wok, heat oil over medium-high heat until a bit of fish skin sizzles immediately when added to oil. Dust fish with cornstarch, shake off excess, and slide fish carefully into oil. Cook, turning once, until both sides are golden brown and a skewer easily penetrates thickest part of meat (about 10 minutes total cooking time per inch of thickness).

5. Lift fish out of oil with spatula, drain a few seconds, and transfer to serving platter. Blot away any excess oil with paper towels and pour sauce over fish. Garnish with fried garlic and coriander.

Serves 4 with other dishes.

Variation Fish may also be deep-fried as in Fried Whole Fish, Nonya Style (see page 44).

A savory sauce of dried mushrooms and ginger graces a delicately pan-fried fish in this Cambodian dish. A steamed version appears on page 68.

Vietnamese banh xeo looks at first like an omelet, but look again—the egg mixture surrounds a crêpelike batter cooked along with the savory pork filling.

PORK-FILLED CRÊPE-OMELETS
Banh xeo
Vietnam

Banh is a Vietnamese word for various flat starch-based foods, including noodles, rice papers, and this unusual combination crêpe and omelet. This recipe will make two large omelets in a 9- or 10-inch skillet or a flat-bottomed wok; you can also make several smaller omelets in a smaller pan or round-bottomed wok.

½ cup rice flour
½ cup thin coconut milk
    (see page 38)
¾ cup water
 6 green onions
    Oil, for stir-frying
½ pound fatty pork, julienned
    (see Note)
 2 cloves garlic, minced
 2 teaspoons fish sauce
    Freshly ground pepper

1 cup bean sprouts
3 eggs, lightly beaten with 3 tablespoons water
Lettuce leaves, for garnish
Sliced cucumber or tomato, for garnish
Mint or coriander leaves, for garnish
Nuoc Leo I or II (see page 36) or Nuoc Mam Sauce (see page 35)

1. In a bowl, combine rice flour, coconut milk, and water and stir until smooth. Batter should be the consistency of rich milk; if necessary, thin with additional water. Slice green onions and add ¼ cup of green tops to batter.

2. In a skillet or flat-bottomed wok, heat about 1 tablespoon oil over medium-high heat (use less oil if using very fatty pork). Add half the pork, half the garlic, and half the remaining green onions and stir-fry until pork is barely done. Season with 1 teaspoon of the fish sauce and pepper. Spread mixture evenly in middle of pan and pour half the batter over it. Scatter half the bean sprouts over the crêpe, then pour half the egg mixture over all, letting it run out beyond the edges of the crêpe.

3. Cover pan and cook until eggs are set and nearly dry (about 3 minutes). Fold omelet in half and transfer to a warm plate.

4. Repeat steps 2 and 3 with remaining filling, batter, and egg mixture. Serve garnished with lettuce, cucumber or tomato, and mint or coriander, and with sauce on the side.

Makes 2 crêpe-omelets, serves 4 with other dishes.

Note Pork belly (uncured bacon) is the usual cut for this dish, but if you prefer a less fatty version use pork shoulder.

Variation Several other fillings are equally delicious. Here are a few. Substitute small raw shrimp, peeled, deveined, and split lengthwise, for all or part of the pork. Add ½ cup sliced mushrooms (fresh button, oyster, dried black, or canned straw mushrooms, or an assortment) to filling along with pork. For a vegetarian filling, use Fried Tofu (see page 44), julienned, in place of the pork, and include one or more of the mushrooms listed above.

CHILE-FRIED SHRIMP
Sambal goreng udang
Indonesia

The amount of chile in this dish can be varied to taste, but bear in mind that sambal dishes are meant to be eaten in small quantities with a lot of rice, not the other way around.

1 pound medium to large shrimp, peeled and deveined
½ teaspoon kosher salt
1 medium onion, finely diced
3 cloves garlic, minced
½ to 1 teaspoon sambal ulek or minced red chile
2 tablespoons oil
1 salam leaf or 2 to 3 curry leaves
½ cup thick coconut milk (see page 38)
1 tablespoon Tamarind Water (see page 34)

1. Sprinkle shrimp with salt and set aside a few minutes while assembling other ingredients. In a mortar or blender, pound onion, garlic, and sambal ulek to a paste.

2. In a wok or skillet, heat oil over medium heat. Add paste and salam leaf and cook until fragrant. Turn heat to medium-high, add shrimp, and stir-fry until they begin to lose their raw color. Add coconut milk and Tamarind Water and continue cooking, stirring constantly, until shrimp are done (another 2 to 3 minutes). Serve hot or at room temperature.

Serves 4 with other dishes.

VIETNAMESE CUISINE

Through a thousand years of Chinese occupation, ending in the tenth century A.D., the Vietnamese managed to assimilate much of Chinese culture yet retain their distinct traditions. On the surface, Vietnam seems the most Chinese-like of the nations of Southeast Asia, with the use of chopsticks, a language that can be written in Chinese characters, and a Confucian social structure. But the food traditions, like the language, remain distinctly Vietnamese. Fish sauce replaces Chinese soy sauce as the common salty condiment. And although the Chinese almost never serve raw vegetables, a platter of raw lettuce, cucumbers, and other vegetables is a part of nearly every Vietnamese meal.

Vietnamese cooks pride themselves on the light, healthful qualities of their food. Simmered and steamed dishes are among the most popular, and stir-fried dishes are cooked with an absolute minimum of oil.

The French occupation of Indochina left its mark on Vietnamese cuisine. A meal might be accompanied by white French bread rather than rice or noodles; men regularly gather in cafés to sip strong, dark coffee; and takeout shops and home cooks alike turn out various forms of pâté—although they are more likely to be steamed or boiled than baked in the European manner.

STIR-FRYING

A variation of pan-frying or sautéing, stir-frying—cooking bite-sized pieces of food quickly over high heat in a small amount of oil, stirring or tossing them constantly—is a technique introduced into Southeast Asian cooking by the Chinese. It has found a place in the repertoire of many non-Chinese cooks as well. As the name implies, the ingredients are stirred constantly during cooking so that they cook evenly. This is an ideal way to preserve the color, flavor, texture, and nutritional value of foods.

Because fuel is scarce in Asia, cooks there have always sought ways of cooking foods with a minimum of fuel. Stir-frying is a perfect example; cutting up the ingredients into small pieces increases the surface area, decreasing the cooking time. In the traditional Southeast Asian kitchen, the heat source was a charcoal fire in a small clay brazier. The fire was fanned until it glowed red-hot, then the food was quickly cooked before the heat died down.

In a modern kitchen where the cooking heat can be controlled with the twist of a knob, the principles of stir-frying remain the same. For busy modern cooks, time is the most precious commodity, and stir-frying is one of the best ways to produce delicious dishes in a short time.

A wok is the ideal pan for stir-frying, but the following recipes can also be prepared in a large skillet. Bear in mind, however, that a flat-bottomed skillet will require more oil to keep the food from sticking.

Because everything happens quickly in stir-frying, organization is essential. Once you start cooking a stir-fried dish, there is no time to cut up the garlic or chile or run to the kitchen cabinet for the fish sauce. So cut, measure, and prepare all the ingredients and assemble the necessary tools and equipment before you turn on the heat. If you hold the dish for any time before serving, turn the oven to a low setting to warm the plate and keep the finished dish.

For best results heat the wok first, then add the oil in a thin stream around the outside of the pan. As the oil slides down the hot sides, it both heats to an ideal cooking temperature and oils the sides to keep the food from sticking. If you accidentally pour in too much oil, don't try to pour it out of the wok. Instead, swab the excess out with a paper towel.

By the time most of the oil has run down into the middle of the wok, it is ready for cooking; if you wait much longer the oil will burn. Scatter the first ingredient to be cooked over the bottom of the pan and immediately begin stirring and tossing with the spatula or with long cooking chopsticks. As you stir, move the more-cooked pieces out of the center and allow the outside pieces to fall in to take their place. Add the remaining ingredients in order of their cooking time, as specified in each recipe, so that all will be finished at once.

Most stir-fried dishes involve some liquid, but it is not added until after the main ingredients have cooked for a while in oil. Adding the liquid too soon will result in braised foods, with a different texture from stir-fried.

Before serving a stir-fried dish, taste a bit. Is the balance of seasonings right? If not, adjust it. Is the sauce reduced the right amount, so that the flavors cling to each bite? If not, reduce it a little further. If the sauce is too thin but the dish is otherwise fully cooked, transfer the meat and vegetables to the serving dish and boil the sauce down before pouring it over.

If your wok has a long handle, it's easy to pour the food out onto the serving platter, scraping the sauce over it with the spatula. If not, scoop the food into the ladle with the spatula and transfer to the serving dish a ladleful at a time. If possible, rinse the wok out immediately with hot water and return it to the heat to dry; otherwise, be sure to wash it as soon as possible.

Because of variations in cookware, heat of the stove, and size of ingredients, it's difficult to specify precise cooking times. Instead, most of the recipes in this chapter give directions such as "cook until fragrant" and "stir-fry until meat loses its raw color." Learn to trust your senses and adjust recipe instructions as needed.

The stir-fry recipes are also not precise on the amount of oil needed, which is usually given simply as "oil, for stir-frying." How much oil to use depends upon the size and condition of your wok (a well-seasoned wok will require less oil to keep foods from sticking), but 1 to 2 tablespoons should be enough in most cases. If the food sticks or seems to be cooking too dry, add a little more oil around the edge of the pan. It will heat up as it slides down the sides.

EGGPLANT WITH PORK AND SHRIMP
Cambodia

This dish falls somewhere between a stir-fry and a stew, as liquid is introduced partway through the cooking. In some versions large eggplant halves are served "stuffed," that is, with the pork mixture heaped on top. Other cooks prefer to cook the eggplant in smaller pieces, as described here.

1 medium eggplant or 3 to 4 slender Japanese eggplants
1 tablespoon oil
1 clove garlic, chopped
½ cup finely ground pork
1 fresh red chile, seeds and veins removed, minced
1 tablespoon soy sauce
½ teaspoon fish sauce
½ teaspoon mild chile powder
1 tablespoon sugar
½ cup Basic Chicken Stock (see page 62)
½ cup water
2 tablespoons Spicy Lime Sauce (see page 35)
½ cup raw shrimp, peeled and chopped
Fresh coriander and sliced green onion, for garnish
Salt and freshly ground pepper, to taste

1. Preheat oven to 450° F. Puncture eggplant in a few places with a fork or skewer. Bake on a sheet pan until soft, about 15 minutes. Set aside and allow to cool slightly, then peel and split lengthwise into strips about 1 inch thick. Eggplant may be baked and peeled up to a day ahead of time.

2. Heat oil in a wok or sauté pan over medium heat. Add garlic and cook until lightly browned. Add pork, chile, soy sauce, fish sauce, chile powder, and sugar and cook, stirring, until meat loses its raw color. Add stock and water and bring to a boil. Add lime sauce, shrimp, and eggplant and simmer until shrimp are done. Transfer eggplant pieces to serving dish and top with pork mixture. Garnish with coriander and green onions.

Serves 4 with other dishes.

LEMONGRASS CHICKEN
Ga xao sa ot
Vietnam

If fresh lemongrass is not available, do not try to substitute the dried or powdered version; the taste won't be the same. Just leave it out; stir-fried chicken with chile and basil is still delicious.

> 2 pounds chicken parts
> 2 stalks lemongrass
> 2 tablespoons fish sauce
> 1 teaspoon sugar
> ½ teaspoon kosher salt
> ¼ teaspoon freshly ground pepper
> 3 green onions, cut into 1-inch pieces
> 1 tablespoon minced garlic
> Oil, for stir-frying
> 2 fresh red chiles, seeded and julienned
> 1 handful fresh basil or mint leaves, or a combination (optional)

1. Chop chicken with a cleaver into braising pieces about 1 inch thick (see page 19). Remove tops and tough outer leaves of lemongrass and slice tender hearts as thin as possible. In a bowl combine chicken, lemongrass, 1 tablespoon of the fish sauce, sugar, salt, pepper, green onions, and garlic and toss to season chicken evenly. Marinate ½ to 1 hour.

2. In a wok or skillet heat oil over medium-high heat. Add chile, stir-fry a few seconds, and add chicken mixture. Stir-fry until chicken shows no trace of pink (about 10 minutes). Add a little water if necessary to prevent scorching. When chicken is done sprinkle with remaining fish sauce, toss with basil or mint if used, and transfer to serving platter.

Serves 4 with other dishes.

Variation Use 1 pound boneless chicken, cut into ¾-inch cubes, and cook over high heat (about 2 or 3 minutes).

Stir-frying is a technique imported from China and adapted to local ingredients. Fragrant lemongrass and mint join with strips of fresh chile to flavor Lemongrass Chicken, a favorite Vietnamese dish.

MEAT-STUFFED SQUID
Vietnam and Cambodia

Wherever in the world squid are cooked, there are cooks who cannot resist stuffing them. The cuisines of Southeast Asia include several versions of stuffed squid. This one uses pork in the stuffing, and the squid are quickly cooked with no sauce. Thai cooks use meat-stuffed squid in a curry, and there is an Indonesian version in which squid stuffed with shrimp are simmered for an hour in a sauce of seasoned coconut milk.

> 1 pound fresh or frozen squid
> ½ pound minced or ground pork (or small cubes if using a blender or food processor)
> 2 cloves garlic
> 2 shallots or 4 green onions
> 6 black mushroom caps or 3 tablespoons cloud ears, soaked and drained
> ¼ cup dried lily flowers, soaked and drained
> ¼ teaspoon freshly ground pepper
> 1 tablespoon fish sauce Pinch salt
> 2 to 3 tablespoons oil Butter lettuce or other tender lettuce leaves

1. Clean squid as directed on page 55, leaving sacs whole. *To prepare by hand:* Chop tentacles, pork, garlic, shallots, mushrooms, and lily flowers finely and combine with pepper, fish sauce, and salt. *To prepare in a blender or food processor:* With motor running, drop whole garlic and shallots in through feed tube. Add mushrooms, pork cubes, squid tentacles, lily flowers, pepper, fish sauce, and salt and grind to a coarse paste, stopping to scrape work bowl occasionally.

2. Using a small spoon or a pastry bag, stuff squid sacs with pork mixture. Fill only halfway to allow for shrinkage of the squid. Close ends with toothpicks. The recipe may be prepared to this point up to 2 hours ahead and refrigerated; remove from refrigerator 15 minutes before cooking.

Stuffed squid is a popular and highly variable dish throughout Southeast Asia. The stuffing may be based on seafood or pork, as in this Indochinese version.

PAN-FRIED SPINACH WITH TWO SAUCES
Cambodia

Because stir-frying is a last-minute process, it is usually not advisable to include more than one stir-fried dish in a menu; but this one is so quick to prepare that you can whip it up while someone is taking the other dishes to the table.

> 2 tablespoons oil
> 1 tablespoon yellow bean sauce
> 1 bunch spinach or watercress, washed and well drained
> 1 teaspoon Chinese oyster sauce

Heat oil almost to smoking in a large skillet or wok. Add bean sauce; cook 15 seconds; add greens. Stir-fry until wilted, stir in oyster sauce, and serve.

Serves 4 with other dishes.

3. In a wok or large skillet, heat oil over medium heat. Add squid and cook, stirring, until they begin to shrink and brown (3 to 4 minutes). Puncture each squid with a skewer or toothpick to release juices (be careful—juice will spatter when it hits the hot oil). Turn heat to high and continue cooking until well browned (another 4 to 5 minutes). Remove pan from heat and cut open a squid to make sure filling is cooked; if not, return pan to heat and continue cooking.

4. Remove toothpicks from finished squid and cut into ½-inch slices. Serve on lettuce leaves.

Serves 4 with other dishes.

Variation Ground beef or dark meat from chicken or turkey may be substituted for pork.

STIR-FRIED VEGETABLES, INDONESIAN STYLE
Tumis
Indonesia

Use an assortment of vegetables for this dish, with an eye toward contrasting colors and textures—cauliflower or broccoli florets; carrots, celery, or green beans, sliced diagonally; red or green bell pepper squares; Chinese or Western-style cabbage, sliced; and so on.

> Oil, for stir-frying
> 1 small onion, sliced
> 1 tablespoon minced garlic
> 3 slices fresh galangal or dried slices soaked in water 30 minutes and drained
> 2 salam leaves or 4 curry leaves
> 1 small fresh chile, seeded and quartered
> 2 cups assorted vegetables
> 2 tablespoons water, if needed
> 1 teaspoon kecap manis, or to taste

1. In a wok or skillet, heat oil over medium heat until a bit of garlic sizzles on contact. Add onion, garlic, galangal, salam leaves, and chile and stir-fry until fragrant.

2. Add vegetables in order of cooking time: Cauliflower takes about 8 minutes, broccoli and carrots about

5 minutes, green beans and celery about 3 minutes, sliced cabbage 1 minute or so. If vegetables are still underdone but onions are in danger of scorching, add water, cover pan, and cook another minute or two.

3. Discard salam leaves and galangal slices and season to taste with kecap manis. Transfer to serving platter.

Serves 4 with other dishes.

SQUID ADOBO
Adobong pusit
Philippines

Most Philippine dishes called adobo are long-simmered stews, like the pork and chicken adobos beginning on page 82. However, this quick-cooking dish is also called an adobo because it features the same basic seasonings of garlic and vinegar. The use of the squid ink is a sign of the Spanish influence on the cuisine of the Philippines.

> 1 pound squid
> ⅓ cup palm or rice vinegar
> 2 tablespoons oil
> 2 tablespoons minced garlic
> Salt and freshly ground pepper

1. Clean squid as directed at right, but reserve entrails. Separate ink sacs, the small silvery organs about an inch long, and place in a fine sieve set over a bowl. Crush ink sacs with a spoon to release ink. Pour vinegar through sieve to extract additional ink; reserve. Discard empty ink sacs and entrails. Cut squid bodies into rings and combine with tentacles.

2. In a wok or skillet, heat oil over medium-low heat. Add garlic and cook slowly until it begins to brown. Turn heat to medium high, add squid, and stir-fry just until they begin to turn opaque (about 30 seconds). Add vinegar mixture and salt and pepper, to taste, turn heat to high, and reduce sauce by half. Correct seasoning and serve with rice.

Serves 4 with other dishes.

Variation Omit ink and add 1 cup peeled, seeded, and diced tomato to pan along with squid.

CLEANING SQUID

1. *Rinse squid in cold water. Cut off tentacles just above eye. Squeeze the thick center part of the tentacles, pushing out the hard beak; discard.*

2. *Squeeze the entrails from the body by running your fingers from the closed to the cut end. Pull out the transparent quill that protrudes from the body.*

3. *Peel off the purple skin if desired. Whole sacs are now ready for slicing or stuffing.*

A VIETNAMESE FAMILY SUPPER

Shrimp and Watercress Soup

*Stir-Fried Mixed Vegetables
With Peanuts*

*Chicken and Rice
in a Clay Pot*

*Nuoc Mam Sauce
(see page 35)*

Tea

*The northern part of
Vietnam, with its cooler
climate and proximity to
China, has a milder cuisine
than that of the hotter
south. This northern-style
menu combines a simple
clear soup, a homey dish of
chicken cooked with rice, the
ever-present Nuoc Mam
Sauce, and crisp stir-fried
vegetables for a satisfying
cool-weather dinner. All
the recipes in this menu
serve four.*

SHRIMP AND WATERCRESS SOUP

This soup can be made either with raw shrimp or with quenelle-like drops of Fresh Shrimp Paste.

> 3 cups Basic Chicken Stock (see page 62)
> 3 green onions, thinly sliced
> 1 tablespoon fish sauce
>   Salt and freshly ground pepper, to taste
> 1 recipe Fresh Shrimp Paste (see page 47) or ½ pound small shrimp, peeled and deveined
> 1 bunch watercress, chopped

1. Bring stock to a boil; reduce to a simmer. Add green onions and fish sauce; season with salt and pepper.

2. *If using shrimp paste:* With a teaspoon dipped in cold water, scoop up a rounded spoonful of paste and drop into soup. Continue with remaining paste, dipping spoon in water between scoops. Simmer until shrimp balls are done (about 4 minutes). *If using whole shrimp:* Add shrimp to soup and simmer until opaque white.

3. Add watercress to soup, simmer until wilted, and serve.

STIR-FRIED MIXED VEGETABLES WITH PEANUTS

Vietnamese stir-frying uses the least amount of oil possible, just enough to keep the foods from sticking; liquid is often added for the final stage of cooking. Reserve a little of the broth from the chicken and rice to use in this dish.

> 1 to 2 tablespoons oil
> 3 green onions, sliced
> 2 stalks celery, sliced diagonally
> 1 medium carrot, julienned
> 2 cups shredded Chinese cabbage
> 2 tablespoons Basic Chicken Stock (see page 62)
> 1 tablespoon fish sauce, or to taste
>   Freshly ground pepper, to taste
> ¼ cup toasted peanuts, coarsely chopped

In a wok or skillet, heat oil over medium-high heat. Add green onions, celery, and carrot and stir-fry 30 seconds. Add cabbage and continue stir-frying until cabbage shreds just begin to soften. Add stock, fish sauce, and pepper, turn heat to high, and cook until liquid is nearly gone. Taste for seasoning and correct if necessary. Transfer to serving platter and garnish with chopped peanuts.

CHICKEN AND RICE IN A CLAY POT
Com tay cam

This simple but satisfying dish is traditionally made in a Chinese-style sandy pot, but any flameproof casserole will do. If using a sandy pot, brown first in a wok or skillet, as these pots cannot withstand direct heat without being filled with liquid.

> 2 shallots, minced
> 2 tablespoons minced garlic
> 1 tablespoon minced ginger
> 2 pounds chicken parts
> 2 tablespoons fish sauce or soy sauce
> 1 or 2 tablespoons oil
>   Freshly ground pepper
> 3 cups water or Basic Chicken Stock (see page 62)
> 8 black mushroom caps, soaked, drained, and halved (reserve soaking liquid)
> 2 cups long-grain rice

1. Combine shallots, garlic, and ginger and mince together as finely as possible, or pound to a paste in a mortar. Disjoint chicken and place in bowl. Add shallot mixture and fish sauce, toss to coat chicken pieces, and marinate 30 minutes.

2. Heat oil in a wok or flame-proof casserole over medium heat. Scrape excess marinade from chicken pieces and cook a few at a time until lightly browned on all sides, removing them as they are done. Add reserved marinade, pepper, water, and reserved mushroom liquid and bring to a boil, scraping up any bits of chicken clinging to pot.

3. Arrange chicken pieces in braising pot and pour in liquid. Cover and simmer until chicken is quite tender (about 20 minutes). Remove chicken from pan and allow to cool. When cool enough to handle, pull or cut meat from bones and cut or tear into thick shreds. Skin can be included or left out, according to taste.

4. Skim excess fat from liquid and add rice and mushrooms. Bring to a boil, reduce heat, and simmer, stirring occasionally, until liquid is nearly absorbed. Taste for seasoning and adjust if necessary. Stir in chicken, cover, and cook over low heat another 10 minutes. Turn off heat and let stand covered 15 minutes. Serve with Nuoc Mam Sauce.

Variation In place of or in addition to the black mushrooms, use 1 cup canned straw mushrooms added along with the shredded chicken. Taste the liquid from the can; if it is not too tinny tasting, use it in place of some of the water or stock.

A delicate clear soup, crisp vegetables studded with chopped peanuts, and a comforting casserole of chicken and rice show the gentle side of Southeast Asian cooking.

The varied techniques of moist-heat cooking yield many favorite foods: delicate soups, succulent steamed dishes, and curries ranging from mild to very hot.

Simmering, Steaming & Stewing

Moist-heat cooking methods—simmering, steaming, and stewing—are an important part of every Southeast Asian cook's skills. Whether the dish is a delicate sour shrimp soup (see page 65), a thick Sumatran beef curry (see page 81), or a fish steamed with mushrooms and preserved plums (see page 71), cooking with moist heat draws together all the flavors of the dish into a satisfying whole. In this chapter you will find recipes and techniques for soups, steamed dishes, curries, and stews from all over Southeast Asia. Tips and recipes starting on page 72 show how to make your own curry pastes, an important first step for many dishes.

MOIST-HEAT COOKING

Compared with cooking with oil or with dry heat, moist-heat cooking is a slow and gentle process, with a more thorough interchange of flavors between the ingredients and the sauce. Simmering or steaming for a relatively short time is one of the best ways to preserve the delicate textures of seafood and tender meats; and longer moist cooking is an ideal way to tenderize tougher cuts of meat.

Slow cooking also gives the cook more flexibility in menu planning. A meal composed entirely of dishes cooked at the last minute can be a logistical nightmare. A better plan is to combine slow- and quick-cooking items; let the cooked rice sit in its covered pan and a curry or soup simmer on the back burner while you prepare a stir-fry or some other last-minute dish.

In all the recipes in this chapter, it is important to remember the distinction between simmering and boiling. Actually, only a few Southeast Asian foods are cooked at a full rolling boil—noodles, for example, or rice in its first stage of cooking. The rest—stocks, soups, stews, and curries—are likely to be superior in flavor, texture, and nutritional value if cooked in liquid that is barely simmering.

The major exception to the above rule is blanching vegetables for salads or dipping. A quick dip in rapidly boiling water, just long enough to fix the color and remove the raw flavor, preserves the flavor and nutrients better than slow cooking. Of course, the water in a steamer should be at a full boil (see page 66).

SOUPS

Southeast Asian soups range from clear broths with a few fragrant ingredients to rich soups based on coconut milk to a hearty bowlful of noodles, vegetables, and meats that can serve as a meal in itself.

Soup is typically served throughout the meal rather than as a first course.

Although other cooked dishes are often served close to room temperature, soup must always be served piping hot. In many homes and restaurants, soup is served in a special pot that is kept warm by its own tabletop burner. A Chinese-style hot pot or fire pot, the type that looks like a baker's tube pan placed over a chimney, is ideal. The heat source may be a canned-alcohol flame or a portable bottled-gas burner. Even a Western-style fondue pot will do. At the very least, the soup will stay warm longer in a covered tureen than in an open bowl.

Many of the recipes in this book call for chicken stock. Unlike a Western-style stock, Asian chicken stock is usually made without a lot of carrots, celery, onions, or herbs. The result is a lighter, "cleaner," more versatile stock (see page 62).

BEEF AND SHRIMP HOT POT
Vietnam

This cook-at-the-table dish is related to the Chinese hot-pot or fire-pot style of cooking, in which the diners cook their own meats in a pot of simmering broth. However, the seasonings of the broth, the soft rice-paper wrappers, and the dipping sauce based on *nuoc mam* make it uniquely Vietnamese.

½ pound tender beef (sirloin or tenderloin)
Freshly ground pepper
1 tablespoon Chinese or Japanese sesame oil
½ pound raw shrimp, peeled and deveined
4 green onions, thinly sliced on the diagonal
1 cup bean sprouts
1 medium cucumber, quartered lengthwise and sliced

½ cup shredded carrots
½ cup shredded cabbage (red, white, or Chinese) or lettuce
1 bunch watercress or coriander, separated into small sprigs
Nuoc Mam Sauce (see page 35)
3 cups water or half water and half Basic Chicken Stock (see page 62) or other light meat broth
1 stalk lemongrass, cut into several pieces and bruised
3 or 4 slices ginger
2 tablespoons rice vinegar or white distilled vinegar
Rice paper

1. Slice beef across grain as thinly as possible (partially freezing the meat first makes it easier to slice thinly). Arrange slices on a platter; sprinkle with pepper and sesame oil. Arrange shrimp on another platter, with green onions piled in the center. Arrange rest of vegetables on another platter.

2. Set each place with a small bowl of water, a bowl of Nuoc Mam Sauce, and chopsticks.

3. Bring water to a boil with lemongrass, ginger, and vinegar. Transfer to a Chinese fire pot, fondue pot, or similar pot that can be kept simmering at the table.

4. To serve, dip a piece of rice paper in water just long enough to soften it, then top it with an assortment of vegetables. With chopsticks, dip a slice of beef or a shrimp and a bit of green onion in the simmering stock until cooked. Roll into rice paper, dip roll in sauce, and eat with fingers. Serve the broth, infused with the flavors of beef and shrimp, as a soup at the end of the meal.

Serves 4 with other dishes.

Variation Other meats and seafoods may be substituted for the beef and shrimp in this recipe: sliced pork loin, chicken breast, scallops, precooked fish balls (see Note to Seafood and Noodles in Coconut Milk, page 63) or small, precooked meatballs made of ground pork or beef.

*In hot-pot cooking, meats and
seafood are cooked at the table in
simmering broth, then folded
with raw vegetables into edible
rice paper and dipped in sauce.*

BASIC CHICKEN STOCK

A simple, lightly flavored chicken stock is one of the essentials of Southeast Asian cooking. The stock may be prepared by simmering or steaming. Traditional recipes often call for a whole chicken, but you can use an assortment of chicken parts. If you buy whole chickens and cut them up yourself, you should have a steady supply of parts available for stock-making. Freeze them until you have accumulated enough for a batch of stock. Do not use livers for stock; other giblets are fine. Also, don't use too many feet or the stock may be too gelatinous for your taste.

Wash thoroughly 2 pounds of chicken parts, bones, or trimmings. If using chicken backs, remove kidneys (the two spongy pink masses along-side the backbone near the tail end) and any other bits of internal organs. Combine chicken with 2 roughly chopped green onions and 3 or 4 slices of ginger.

1. *To prepare by steaming (see photo above):* Place chicken parts, green onions, and ginger slices with water to cover in a deep bowl that will fit inside a large stockpot. Place bowl inside pot, elevated on a steaming rack. Add water to pot to a depth of at least 2 inches (bowl can be partly immersed). Bring to a boil, reduce heat so that water simmers, and steam covered 1 to 3 hours.

To prepare by simmering: Place chicken parts in a stockpot and cover with water by 2 inches or so. Bring to a boil, then reduce to a simmer, and skim off any foam that comes to the surface. Add green onions and ginger slices and simmer 1 to 3 hours, skimming occasionally.

2. Turn off heat and let stock settle a few minutes, then ladle or pour stock through a fine strainer (see photo above). Leave behind the last ½ cup or so that will be full of sediment. For perfectly clear stock, strain through several thicknesses of moistened cheesecloth.

Rich Chicken Stock A few recipes call for a rich stock, which can be made in one of two ways. The first is to add pork or veal bones and trimmings (beef gives too strong a flavor for this purpose) to the Basic Chicken Stock recipe above. Increase the simmering time by an hour or more to extract additional flavor and body.

The second way to make a rich stock is to follow the basic recipe, but begin with a previous batch of stock in place of water. The resulting double stock makes an excellent soup. If you cut up chickens regularly, this is a good way to keep a batch of stock fresh, and it gets richer with each extraction. Rich stock can always be diluted with water when a basic or thin stock is called for.

To Store Stock Allow stock to cool, then refrigerate covered or freeze. Refrigerated stock may be kept 2 or 3 days, longer if brought to a boil for 10 minutes every other day. Frozen stock will keep for months.

SEAFOOD AND NOODLES IN COCONUT MILK
Laksa
Malaysia and Indonesia

Not all Indonesian and Malay dishes are hot, as this gentle soup demonstrates. *Laksa* may be made with chicken or various types of seafood, but all versions are based on coconut milk and include either rice sticks or bean threads. Of course, if you want it to be hotter, you can always add a little Sambal Bajak (see page 37) to your bowl.

- ¼ cup minced onion or shallot
- 2 cloves garlic, minced
- 1 tablespoon minced ginger
- 3 macadamia nuts, chopped (optional)
- 2 teaspoons ground coriander
- ½ teaspoon each *ground caraway and turmeric*
  Pinch ground chile
- 1 tablespoon oil
- 1 stalk lemongrass, cut into several pieces and bruised
- 2 cups each *thick and thin coconut milk (see page 38)*
- 1 cup coconut cream skimmed from the thick coconut milk (optional)
  Salt, to taste
- 1 pound assorted seafood, any combination of the following: cooked and peeled shrimp; cooked, flaked crabmeat; fish balls (see Note), squid, cleaned (see page 55) and cut into bite-sized pieces; steamed and shucked mussels or Manila clams; halibut or other firm fish, in ½-inch cubes
- ½ pound rice sticks, cooked
- 1 cup bean sprouts
  Fried Onion Flakes (see page 35), for garnish

1. *To prepare in a mortar:* Pound onion, garlic, ginger, and nuts (if used) to a paste and stir in ground coriander, caraway, turmeric, and chile. *To prepare in a blender or food processor:* Combine ingredients listed above with coconut cream and blend until smooth.

2. In a saucepan or wok, heat oil over medium heat (omit oil if paste was blended with coconut cream). Add paste and lemongrass and cook, stirring constantly, until mixture is quite fragrant. Add coconut milk, bring just to a boil, and reduce to a simmer. Salt soup to taste.

3. Add seafoods to simmering soup in order of cooking time. Fish balls and cubes take about 5 minutes to cook; cooked shellfish need just a few minutes to reheat; and squid cooks in about 30 seconds.

4. Place rice sticks and bean sprouts in a soup tureen or in individual bowls and add soup. Garnish each bowl with onion flakes.

Serves 4 to 6 with other dishes.

Note Fish balls made of finely ground lean fish are available fresh and frozen in Asian markets. To make your own, remove all the bones and skin from fillets or steaks of lean fish and chop to a paste in a food processor or grind through the finest disk of a meat grinder. With hands dipped in cold water, roll into 1-inch balls and refrigerate covered for 1 to 6 hours before cooking.

Variation Substitute diced boneless chicken (light or dark meat) for the seafood.

BEEF SOUP WITH NOODLES
Pho bo
Vietnam

Restaurants specializing in *pho,* a sort of soup-plus-salad served in a single bowl, are found in many Vietnamese cities, and they are an increasingly common sight in Vietnamese neighborhoods in this country as well. Pho (pronounced more or less *far*) is traditionally served for breakfast, but it is equally good to eat for lunch or a light supper.

5 pounds meaty beef bones (ribs, neck, or shank)
1 pound boneless stewing beef (chuck or short ribs—see Note)
1 cinnamon stick
3 pods star anise
1 medium onion, sliced (include skin if clean)
10 to 12 slices fresh ginger
 Salt or fish sauce, to taste
½ pound tender beef (sirloin or flatiron—see Note)
2 cups bean sprouts
2 or 3 fresh chiles, sliced
2 medium tomatoes, cut into wedges (optional)
 Lemon or lime wedges
 Sprigs of fresh coriander, mint, or basil
½ pound rice sticks, cooked, or ¾ pound Fresh Rice Noodles, prepared as directed on page 109, cooked
1 medium onion, sliced as thinly as possible
 Liquid chile sauce

1. Rinse bones and place in a large stockpot. Cover amply with cold water. Bring to a boil and cook 15 minutes, skimming off foam that rises to the surface. When foaming stops, add stewing beef, cinnamon, star anise, onion, and ginger. Reduce heat so stock barely simmers and cook from 6 to 12 hours. Begin checking stewing beef after an hour or so and remove when quite tender but not yet falling apart.

2. Strain stock and skim off and discard fat from surface. Season to taste with salt or fish sauce. Stock may be prepared up to 3 days ahead and stored uncovered in the refrigerator.

3. Bring stock to a boil. Slice stewed and raw beef thinly across the grain. Arrange bean sprouts, chiles, tomatoes (if used), lemon wedges, and herbs on a platter or individual plates. Warm deep soup bowls with hot water. Place some rice sticks in each bowl and top with cooked and raw beef and sliced onion. Ladle hot stock over all (heat of stock will cook raw beef). Serve immediately, each person adding vegetables, herbs, chiles, fish sauce, and liquid chile sauce to taste. Serve with both chopsticks and a soup spoon.

Serves 6 to 8.

Note Blade chuck roast or steak is often a good buy, and if you bone it yourself it can provide both the stewing and the tender cuts for this dish. Look for a 3-pound roast or a couple of steaks with a long, slender blade bone. The flatiron muscle on top of the blade bone (the opposite side from the ribs and backbone) is tender enough for quick cooking, but the remaining muscles require longer cooking. The rib eye, the large round muscle alongside the ribs, falls somewhere between in tenderness, and is best reserved for another use, such as a Thai curry. Add the bones to the stockpot.

Variation I Other cuts of beef, including organ meats, can be used in place of the stewing beef. Tripe is especially good to use this way. If shanks are used for the stock, the shank meat can be sliced and included in the soup. One of the most popular items in *pho* restaurants is beef tendons, which become tender and gelatinous when simmered in the stock for many hours.

Variation II A similar soup may be made from chicken, in which case it is called *pho ga.* Use a 4- to 5-pound stewing fowl with giblets (but omit the liver), and half the amount of spices and ginger. Simmer for only 2 to 3 hours. Remove the cooked meat and shred it by hand, then assemble the soup as directed above, with some sliced giblets in each bowl.

The Indonesian version of chicken-noodle soup is soto ayam, a fragrant bowl of chicken shreds, bean threads, and assorted vegetables seasoned to each diner's taste with lime juice and chile.

SPICY CHICKEN SOUP WITH GARNISHES
Soto ayam
Indonesia

"Chicken soup" is the literal translation of *soto ayam*, but it hardly does justice to this dish. Whether you serve it as the main dish for a casual meal or as part of an elaborate banquet, it is a do-it-yourself affair—each diner assembles a bowl of chicken shreds, vegetables, and bean threads, ladles over it a chicken broth fragrant with lemongrass and spices, and seasons it to taste with lime juice and a hot chile sambal.

   1 *chicken, about 4 pounds*
   1 *medium onion, diced*
   2 *tablespoons each minced ginger and garlic*
   1 *stalk lemongrass, sliced or 1 tablespoon dried flakes*
   2 *teaspoons ground coriander*
   1 *teaspoon ground cumin*
 1½ *teaspoons each freshly ground black pepper and galangal*
   1 *teaspoon sugar*
   1 *cup shredded cabbage or Chinese cabbage*
  ¼ *pound bean threads, soaked in hot water until soft and transparent*
   1 *cup diced red bell pepper or peeled and diced tomato*
     Lime or lemon wedges
     Cucumber slices
     Salt, to taste
     Sambal Bajak (see page 37) or sambal ulek

1. Clean and disjoint the chicken (see page 18). In a large saucepan cover chicken parts with cold water and bring to a boil. Reduce heat slightly and cook 5 minutes, skimming foam from the surface.

2. When foaming stops, add onion, ginger, garlic, and lemongrass. (If using whole spices, toast coriander and cumin before grinding.) Add to soup with black pepper, galangal, and sugar. Simmer until chicken is tender (about 45 minutes).

3. When chicken is done, remove parts from soup and let stand until cool enough to handle. Pull meat off bones and return bones to pot. Shred meat by hand or with a knife and place in the middle of a platter.

4. Blanch cabbage in boiling water for 30 seconds and transfer to platter with a slotted spoon or Chinese wire strainer. Drain bean threads, cut into manageable lengths, and place on platter. Arrange bell pepper, cucumber, and lime wedges on platter.

5. Skim excess fat from soup, salt soup to taste, and strain into a heated tureen. For each serving, combine some chicken shreds, bean threads, cabbage, cucumbers, and peppers in a bowl and ladle in the hot soup. Squeeze in lime juice and add sambal to taste.

Serves 4 to 6 as a main dish, 8 to 12 as a first course.

Variation For additional flavor, the shredded chicken can be marinated for 10 minutes in 2 tablespoons Tamarind Water (see page 34), drained, and stir-fried in oil until lightly browned.

TWO SOUR SEAFOOD SOUPS

A recurring theme throughout Southeast Asian cuisines is a seafood soup with a refreshing sour ingredient such as lemongrass, citrus juice, citrus leaves, or tamarind. In some versions the flavor is noticeably sour, while in others there is more of a lemony aroma than actual acidity. Here are two examples drawn from different cuisines. The Thai Sour Shrimp Soup is the most intricately flavored, with lemongrass, lime juice, and Kaffir lime leaves, each adding their own flavor and aroma. The thick Burmese Fish Chowder With Rice Sticks uses a small amount of lime juice to balance the strong flavors of garlic, turmeric, and shrimp paste. Other cuisines have sour fish soups, too. Indonesian and Philippine versions often rely on tamarind, and in Laos and southern Vietnam, the ingredient is often pickled bamboo shoots.

SOUR SHRIMP SOUP
Tom yam kung
Thailand

This soup can be made mild or incendiary or anywhere in between by varying the amount of chile and the way it is used. This version is fairly tame. For a hotter flavor, mince some of the chiles and pound them in with the seasoning paste. For a more substantial soup, soak 2 to 3 ounces rice sticks or bean threads in warm water until soft and add to soup or place in individual bowls.

> 1 pound shrimp, preferably with heads
> 1 quart water or Basic Chicken Stock (see page 62)
> 1 stalk lemongrass
> 1 tablespoon minced coriander root
> ½ teaspoon peppercorns
> 2 cloves garlic, peeled
> 1 or 2 fresh chiles, split lengthwise, loose seeds removed
> 2 Kaffir lime leaves
> Juice of 1 lime
> 1 cup sliced mushrooms (optional)
> Fish sauce, to taste
> Coriander leaves or sliced green onions, for garnish

1. Peel shrimp, reserving shells and heads if any. Devein if necessary. In a saucepan, combine heads and shells with water and simmer 15 minutes. Cut top of lemongrass stalk into 2-inch sections, pound lightly with side of knife blade, and add to stock. Slice remaining lemongrass as finely as possible.

2. In a mortar or blender, combine sliced lemongrass, coriander root, peppercorns, and garlic and pound to a paste. Moisten with a little of the lime juice if necessary.

3. Strain stock and discard shells and lemongrass tops. Return stock to pan and add paste, chiles, lime leaves, and lime juice. Simmer 5 minutes, add shrimp and mushrooms (if used), and simmer until shrimp turns pink and opaque. Season to taste with fish sauce and garnish with coriander leaves.

Serves 4 to 6.

Sour Fish Soup *(Tom yam pla)*
Use slices or cubes of any lean, mild-flavored fish in place of the shrimp.

FISH CHOWDER WITH RICE STICKS
Moo hin nga
Burma

Mashing the cooked fish to a paste gives a thick consistency to this soup, and ground toasted rice also adds thickening.

> 1 tablespoon minced ginger
> ¼ cup minced onion or shallot
> 2 tablespoons minced garlic
> 1 teaspoon shrimp paste
> ¾ teaspoon mild ground chile or ½ teaspoon paprika and ¼ teaspoon cayenne
> Pinch turmeric
> 2 tablespoons oil
> 3 cups thin coconut milk (see page 38)
> 1 pound fish fillets or steaks
> Juice of 1 lime
> 2 tablespoons Toasted Rice Powder (see below)
> Salt or fish sauce, to taste
> Liquid hot-pepper sauce, to taste (optional)
> 2 ounces rice sticks, boiled just until soft and then drained and cooled
> Sliced hard-cooked eggs, for garnish (optional)
> Coriander leaves, for garnish (optional)

Toasted Rice Powder

> 2 tablespoons uncooked rice (long or short grain)

1. In a mortar or blender, pound ginger, onion, and garlic to a paste and blend in shrimp paste, ground chile, and turmeric.

2. In a saucepan or wok, heat oil over medium-low heat and fry paste until quite fragrant. Add coconut milk, fish, and lime juice, bring almost to a boil, reduce heat, and simmer until fish is done.

3. Remove fish with a slotted spoon and drain. Remove skin and bones, if any. Cut half the fish into bite-sized pieces and set aside. Pound the remaining fish to a paste in a mortar, or place in a bowl and mash with a fork until smooth. Soup and fish may be prepared to this point ahead of time and covered and refrigerated.

4. Add rice powder to soup, bring to a boil, and simmer until thickened. Season to taste with salt. If a hotter flavor is desired, add liquid hot-pepper sauce. Add diced and pounded fish. Place rice sticks in soup tureen or individual bowls and ladle in soup. Garnish with hard-cooked eggs and coriander.

Serves 4 with other dishes.

Toasted Rice Powder In a small dry skillet, toast rice to a light tan color, shaking pan constantly so grains brown evenly. Transfer to a mortar, electric spice grinder, or blender with a 1-cup jar and grind to a powder.

CHICKEN AND COCONUT MILK SOUP
Tom ka kai
Thailand

This soup is found on the menu of virtually every Thai restaurant in this country. The bright flavors of lemongrass, chile, and galangal, which is called *ka* in Thai, combine beautifully with the rich, round flavor of the coconut milk. Adjust the amounts of chile and lime to taste, but don't make the soup too hot or too sour, or the balance of flavors will be upset.

> 2 *cups thin coconut milk (see page 38)*
> 2 *pounds chicken parts, cut into braising pieces (see page 19)*
> 8 *slices fresh or dried galangal, soaked in warm water 15 minutes*
> 1 *stalk lemongrass, cut into 2-inch lengths and bruised*
> 4 *Kaffir lime leaves*
> 1 *or 2 fresh chiles, split lengthwise, loose seeds removed*
> 1 *cup thick coconut milk*
> ½ *teaspoon kosher salt*
> 2 *tablespoons each fish sauce and lime juice, or to taste Fresh coriander, for garnish (optional)*

1. In a saucepan, combine thin coconut milk, chicken, galangal, lemongrass, lime leaves, and chiles. Bring to a boil, reduce heat, and simmer until chicken is tender, about 30 minutes. Soup may be prepared to this point ahead of time and refrigerated.

2. Just before serving, add thick coconut milk, salt, fish sauce, and lime juice and bring just to a boil. Simmer a few minutes longer and transfer to a heated soup tureen or individual bowls. Garnish with coriander leaves if desired.

Serves 4 to 6.

Variation For a quick version, eliminate the chicken parts in step 1 and substitute Basic Chicken Stock (page 62) for 1 cup of the thin coconut milk. Simmer ten minutes, add diced boneless meat of 1 chicken breast, and proceed with step 2.

STEAMED DISHES

Steaming—cooking food over rather than in boiling liquid—is one of the most useful of cooking techniques. It is an excellent method in terms of nutrition; where vitamins might be washed away during boiling, steaming keeps vitamin loss to a minimum. Steamed vegetables keep their color better than those that are boiled or cooked in oil. Steaming is also efficient; a stacking steamer set allows many different foods to be stacked and cooked at once over one heat source. It is also an ideal way to reheat leftovers, cooking them quickly without adding or subtracting liquid. But the greatest virtue of steaming is in the texture and flavor of the finished dish. There is no better way to preserve the delicate taste and texture of a fresh fish than to cook it gently with steam.

Steaming apparatus comes in all sizes and shapes, from specially designed pots to wok accessories. All are designed to support food over boiling water, with room for steam to circulate around the food.

A wok with a dome-shaped cover is adequate for occasional steaming. Most wok sets include a steaming rack of some sort that fits inside the wok and holds a plate above the water line. Chinese-style bamboo steamer baskets an inch or two smaller than the wok need no other support, and they can be stacked on one another, allowing you to cook several different items over one pot of water. All the steaming recipes in this chapter can be made in a standard 14-inch wok with a cover and either type of steaming rack.

The wok has some disadvantages as a steamer. Its round-bottomed design is a handicap, holding less water than a straight-sided pot, so it may boil dry before the job is done. Also, since steaming is hard on the surface of a well-seasoned wok, you always need to reseason it, both to avoid rust and to help in stir-frying.

If you do a lot of steaming, a metal stacking steamer set is a convenience, freeing your wok for other uses. Asian markets carry these sets in various sizes and designs. A typical set consists of a lightweight metal pot at least 5 inches deep with two or more perforated stacking trays and a cover. For convenience and flexibility, choose the largest size to fit on your stove; 12 inches is about the minimum diameter to consider.

Small quantities of food can be steamed in a covered pan with a round folding steamer rack, an inexpensive item sold in most cookware shops. If the rack does not have a central post, it can hold a bowl or plate. Pots with perforated steaming inserts will also do for vegetables or a few Rice Packets (see page 104) or other banana-leaf packages.

Caution Steam can cause severe burns. When lifting the cover off a steaming pot, open it away from you and let the steam dissipate before reaching or looking inside. Long sleeves or long oven mitts will prevent steam burns on wrists.

STEAMING IN BANANA LEAVES

Southeast Asian foods are often wrapped in leaves before steaming. Banana leaves are the favorite, as they grow throughout the region. Frozen banana leaves from the Philippines are available in some Asian markets, and they keep well after thawing. Ti leaves from Hawaii, available through florists, are smaller but can be used in a similar way. Although the leaves are not eaten, they give a subtle fragrance to the foods cooked inside. You can substitute aluminum foil, but that special aroma will be missing.

In the following recipes the food to be steamed is first wrapped in a rectangular package. Here's how: Start with a piece of banana leaf about 12 inches square (pouring boiling water over it first makes it more pliable). With the fibers of the leaf horizontal, place the food in the center of the square, allowing at least 4 inches of leaf on all sides. Fold the near and far edges over the food, forming a tube. Fold the ends of the tube over the top and secure with a toothpick, or tie with string or a strip of leaf. Banana leaves split easily, so start with more than you think you will need, and handle them carefully.

Foods that have been cooked in leaves may be served in their packages, or you can unwrap them in the kitchen. For a nice presentation, spread out one of the wrappers on the serving platter and add the contents of the other packages.

To substitute foil for banana leaves, fold into a tube shape as described above, but seal the ends by rolling them up rather than by folding them over the top. Toothpicks and string are unnecessary.

STEAMED CATFISH IN BANANA LEAVES
Malaysia and Indonesia

Many supermarkets now carry farm-raised catfish in pan-ready form, with the head and skin removed. If you buy catfish in an Asian market, it will probably come with the skin and head on. Cut off and save the head for soup. The skin can be left on the steaks, although it will curl up a bit.

> Banana leaves
> 1½ to 2 pounds pan-ready catfish
> Tamarind Water (see page 34), made with 1 tablespoon prepared tamarind pulp and 2 tablespoons water
> ¼ teaspoon turmeric
> ¼ cup thinly sliced onion
> 3 cloves garlic, sliced
> 1 tablespoon minced fresh green or red chile
> 2 teaspoons shredded ginger
> Pinch salt
> 1 stalk lemongrass, cut into 1½-inch lengths and bruised
> ½ cup peeled, seeded, and diced tomato

1. Pour hot water over banana leaves to soften them; drain and set aside.

2. Cut catfish crosswise through bones into ¾-inch-thick steaks; leave tail sections whole. Place in a bowl,

add Tamarind Water, turmeric, onion, garlic, chile, ginger, and salt, and toss to season evenly. Cover bowl and marinate 1 to 3 hours in refrigerator.

3. Lay out 4 squares of banana leaf and divide fish pieces evenly among them. Top each portion with marinade ingredients, lemongrass, and tomato. Fold leaves into packages as directed on page 66 and seal with toothpicks.

4. Bring water in steamer to a rolling boil. Place fish packages seam side up in steamer basket or on steaming plate and steam 15 minutes.

Serves 4 with other dishes.

Sealed in banana-leaf packages with aromatic vegetables and then steamed, catfish develops a special succulence and flavor. Other mild-flavored fish may be prepared the same way.

STEAMED FISH WITH GINGER-MUSHROOM SAUCE
Mudcha troug kroeung
Cambodia

This sauce is equally delicious on deep-fried or pan-fried fish (see page 48 for a pan-fried version). For a variety of flavors and textures, use an assortment of mushrooms such as fresh button or oyster mushrooms, dried Chinese black mushrooms, and canned straw mushrooms.

> 1 whole catfish, rockfish, snapper, or flounder, prepared as directed on page 19
> ¼ cup Tamarind Water (see page 34)
> 1 teaspoon sugar
> ½ cup Basic Chicken Stock (see page 62)
> Dash black soy sauce or kecap manis
> 2 tablespoons oil
> 1 tablespoon dried garlic flakes, for garnish
> 2 tablespoons finely shredded fresh ginger
> 1 teaspoon yellow bean sauce
> ¼ cup assorted sliced mushrooms
> 1 tablespoon dried shrimp
> 1 green onion, cut into 2-inch lengths
> ¼ cup sliced yellow onion
> 1 ounce bean threads, soaked until soft and drained (optional)

1. Score sides of fish and place on a plate that will fit inside your steamer. Bring water in steamer to a rolling boil, add fish, and steam until a skewer easily penetrates the thickest part, about 15 to 20 minutes. While fish is steaming, prepare sauce (steps 2 and 3).

2. In a small saucepan, combine Tamarind Water and sugar and bring to a boil. Reduce to 2 tablespoons, remove from heat, and add stock and soy sauce.

3. Heat oil in a skillet over low heat. Fry garlic flakes and set aside. Turn heat to medium-high, add ginger and

yellow bean sauce, and cook until fragrant. Add mushrooms, dried shrimp, and green and yellow onions and cook until vegetables soften. Add stock mixture and bean threads, if used, and bring to a boil. Reduce by half, taste for seasoning, and pour over fish. Garnish with fried garlic.

Serves 4 with other dishes.

Variation In place of the whole fish, use steaks or fillets of similar fish and reduce the cooking time to approximately 10 minutes per inch of thickness.

CURRIED CHICKEN STEAMED IN BANANA LEAVES

This is a hybrid dish, combining the Laotian technique of steaming chicken in leaves with the flavors of a Thai curry. It may not be authentic, but it tastes good.

> Banana leaves, cut into 12-inch squares
> 2 pounds chicken parts, disjointed or cut into braising pieces (see page 19)
> 1 tablespoon fish sauce
> ½ cup thick coconut milk (see page 38)
> 1 to 2 tablespoons red, green, or yellow curry paste (see pages 74 to 75)
> Kaffir lime leaves

1. Pour hot water over banana leaves to soften them; drain and set aside.

2. Sprinkle chicken pieces with fish sauce and let stand 5 minutes. In a wok or skillet, heat coconut milk and curry paste over low heat until mixture begins to bubble. Remove from heat and allow to cool.

3. Toss chicken pieces in curry mixture to coat. Place 1 or more pieces in the middle of a square of banana leaf, spoon over some more of the curry mixture, and top with a lime leaf. Fold banana leaf into a rectangular package (see page 66) and seal with toothpicks. Place in steamer, seam side up, and steam 45 minutes.

Serves 4 with other dishes.

STEAMING VEGETABLES

A simple steamed vegetable is often the perfect counterpart to intricately seasoned Southeast Asian dishes. Since steaming is essentially a hands-off cooking method, it leaves you free to put the finishing touches on other dishes. Rather than specific recipes, here are some suggestions for vegetables for steaming and tips for getting the best results.

Be careful when combining vegetables, as they do not all cook at the same rate. Steaming mixed vegetables of about the same density, such as cauliflower, broccoli, and carrots, works fine; but to cook cauliflower and zucchini together would be a disaster—the zucchini would be an olive-green mush by the time the cauliflower was ready.

Sauces and seasonings should be determined by the rest of the menu. In most cases, no sauce is necessary. Cabbage tastes especially good steamed in a bowl with a salty ingredient such as dark soy sauce, yellow bean sauce, or dried shrimp. Other ingredients can be sprinkled on top of cooked vegetables: Try crisp-fried bits of garlic or shallot on green beans, toasted grated coconut on broccoli, or ground dried shrimp on just about anything. And of course, steamed vegetables are delicious dipped in Nuoc Mam Sauce, or one of the other table sauces on page 35.

You don't need a special steaming pot for plain steamed vegetables; a folding round steamer rack that fits inside a covered saucepan will work fine. In fact, this setup does a faster job of steaming a few vegetables than a large steamer set.

Cauliflower Remove outside leaves and cut florets away from base. For best appearance, do not cut through florets from outside; instead, separate or split stems and break apart into bite-sized pieces.

Broccoli Look for stalks with fairly small bases, which will not need peeling. Starting at the base, cut stem into ¼-inch-thick slices; continue cutting until florets fall away from central stem. The slender, small-flowered Chinese broccoli can be cut, leaves and all, into 2-inch or longer sections.

Summer Squash Cut zucchini, crookneck, or similar shapes into thick sticks; steam only until heated through or they will become mushy. The related chayote, also known as vegetable pear or mirliton, is similar in flavor but takes longer to cook.

Potatoes, Yams, Sweet Potatoes Scrub rather than peel unless skins are very tough; cut into ¾-inch cubes. Cook them just until centers are tender.

Green Beans Remove tops and strings if necessary and cut into desired length. Chinese long beans can take a surprisingly long time to cook fully.

Peas Freshly shelled or frozen peas need just a few minutes in the steamer.

Snow Peas, Sugar Snap Peas Steam in the pods with a little finely shredded onion or shallot.

Cabbages Cut globe types into thick wedges, then into cubes; handle carefully before cooking so they do not fall apart. Steam just until bright green. Cut bok choy stems crosswise into 1-inch pieces, leaves into larger squares; cook until stems are done but still crunchy and leaves are limp. Chinese (Napa) cabbage is better cooked by simmering or stir-frying.

Asparagus Although it is not common in Asia, fresh asparagus steamed until just tender is quite at home in a Southeast Asian meal, especially when you are eating with your fingers.

Steaming is the ideal way to preserve the goodness of fresh seasonal vegetables. Asian-style stacking steamers are useful but not essential.

In this Thai presentation, a single pomfret—a fish similar to our pompano—is split in half, boned, laid out to resemble two fish, and steamed.

STEAMED BONELESS POMFRET
Pla nueng
Thailand

Pomfret is a popular saltwater fish throughout Southeast Asia, similar in appearance and flavor to our pompano. It is available frozen in Asian markets. You can use the sauce and cutting technique described here on pompano, butterfish, smaller species of jack, or even very fresh mackerel. This recipe is courtesy of Chalie Amatyakul, director, Thai Cooking School at the Oriental, Bangkok.

> 1   whole pomfret or pompano (1½ to 2 lb), with head
> 6   black mushroom caps, soaked, drained, and cut in half (reserve liquid)
> 2   Chinese salt-preserved plums, soaked until soft and drained (discard liquid)
> 2   tablespoons shredded ginger
> 1   tablespoon each *chopped garlic and coriander root*
> 1   tablespoon dark soy sauce Pinch freshly ground pepper
> 2   ounces fatty pork, chopped (optional)
> 1   green onion, shredded, for garnish
> 1   or 2 tablespoons oil (less if using pork)

1. Prepare fish as shown in Steaming Whole Fish, at right. Arrange as shown in step 3, with mushroom caps between slices of fillet.

2. Mash plums and remove pits. Combine with mushroom liquid, ginger, garlic, coriander root, soy sauce, pepper, and pork, if used. Spread mixture over fish. Steam until just done, about 10 minutes. Garnish with green onion.

3. Heat oil in a small skillet or saucepan and pour over fish. Serve immediately.

Serves 2 to 4 with other dishes.

Variation The same sauce can be used on a whole fish, as in Steamed Fish with Ginger-Mushroom Sauce (see page 68). Use half again as much sauce for a 2- to 3-pound fish. Leave the mushroom caps whole or cut them into strips.

Step·by·Step

STEAMING WHOLE FISH

Cooking a whole fish gently with steam is an ideal way to preserve its delicate taste and texture. All over Southeast Asia, a whole fish steamed in the Chinese manner is a popular restaurant dish. One might expect that each country would have its own version, using favorite local ingredients, but this is not the case.

Most versions closely resemble one Chinese variation or another, and they tend to stick to the same seasonings: ginger, green onion, soy sauce, fermented bean sauces, and sometimes minced pork (also common in Chinese recipes). A Nonya cook in Singapore might use a little more fresh chile than a cook in Canton or Shanghai, but otherwise the dish would be similar.

In some versions, such as the Steamed Boneless Pomfret pictured at left, the sauce ingredients are steamed along with the fish; in others, such as Steamed Fish With Ginger-Mushroom Sauce (see page 68), a sauce is prepared separately and poured over the finished fish.

If possible steam the fish on the plate on which it will be served; this eliminates the danger of the cooked fish coming apart when it is transferred out of the steamer. Make sure that the combination of pot, plate, and cover will fit together before bringing the water to a boil.

In the following photos, a boneless fish is prepared to look like a whole fish—two fish, in fact.

1. Have the fish cleaned, with the head left on. With a stiff-bladed knife, cut apart head, tail, middle pieces—along with their supporting bones—and upper and lower fins.

2. Split head in half, and set it aside. Cut fillets free from bones with long, smooth strokes. Discard bones.

3. Cut fillets into 3 or 4 pieces each. Arrange both fillets skin side up on plate with other ingredients. Add head, tail, and fins in position. Steam on a plate in a wok or in a steamer pan.

CURRIES AND STEWS

A great number of the simmered and stewed dishes of Southeast Asia come under the general heading of "curries." Although Westerners often think of curry as a single flavor, that of the Indian-style curry powder, it is actually a cooking method rather than an ingredient. In fact, all "curry" means, in all its regional forms from India and Pakistan to Indonesia, is a dish of meat, seafood, or vegetables cooked in a seasoned liquid.

Most of the cuisines of Southeast Asia include curried dishes, but the greatest variety is found in Burma, Thailand, Malaysia, and the western islands of Indonesia. These curries are typically based on coconut milk, infused with the flavors of a highly seasoned paste. The sauce may be thin and soupy or reduced until thick and clinging.

Burmese curries show a stronger Indian influence than those of other countries, with spices like cumin and cardamom playing an important role. Thai curries come in a range of colors and flavors, with yellow curries (colored with turmeric) generally the mildest and red and green curries (made with dried and fresh chiles, respectively) the hottest. The most famous Malay curry is that of Penang, a thick, highly spiced red curry thickened with ground peanuts (see page 81). Indonesian curries generally rely less on the intense heat of chiles and more on ground spices and aromatic roots.

A traditional reason for cooking meats with chiles and other spices was to preserve them, especially in tropical regions without refrigeration. With modern refrigeration, we do not need to be so concerned with keeping meat from spoiling; however, curries still keep well, and many cooks prefer to make them a day or two ahead of serving to allow the flavors to deepen. This is especially true of curries made with larger cubes of meat or poultry, such as Beef Curry, Sumatra Style (see page 81), or Burmese Dry Pork Curry (see page 78).

Not all the stewed dishes of Southeast Asian cooking are curries, however. Vietnamese cooks make delicately flavored stews of beef, pork, and poultry with few of the seasonings typical of curries. The Philippine pot roast and the vinegar-based adobos (see pages 82–83) are also examples of stews other than curries.

For a special presentation of any of the curries in this book, try serving them inside a coconut. For best results use an immature or green coconut (shown cracked open in photograph on page 39). These young, soft-fleshed coconuts, shipped by air from Hawaii, are now available in well-stocked produce markets. Lay the coconut on its side. With a heavy knife or cleaver, cut through the outer husk about one third of the way from the top to form a removable lid. The cut should take off the top inch or so of the inner shell, leaving a hole about 4 inches in diameter. Pour out the juice and reserve for another use, if desired. Ladle the finished curry into the coconut, replace the lid, and stand the coconut up in a small bowl that fits inside a tall steaming pot (a pasta pot is ideal). Steam 15 minutes and serve in the shell, scooping out pieces of the soft coconut flesh along with the curry. Note that most of the curry recipes in this book make more than can fit inside a single coconut; the rest can be served in a bowl or used to refill the coconut.

CURRY PASTES

The flavor foundation of a Thai, Malay, or Indonesian curry (and many other dishes as well) is a mixture of spices, herbs, and aromatic vegetables ground together to a paste. Curry pastes are traditionally pounded by hand in a mortar, and purists say this still gives the best texture and flavor to the paste; but many modern cooks prefer to use a blender or food processor.

Whichever method you use, here are a few basic rules to keep in mind. The first is to start with whole ingredients whenever possible. Drying, grinding, and otherwise processing ingredients for long storage changes the flavors and aromas. Ground spices, for example, quickly lose the volatile oils that give them their distinctive flavors. Whole spices can last for many months or even years, but ground, they will fade within a few months. Freshly peeled garlic and ginger have a totally different flavor from their dried, flaked, or ground equivalents.

When it is necessary to begin with dried ingredients, such as galangal or dried Kaffir lime peel, it is best to buy them in the largest possible pieces and grind them to order. Thick slices of dried galangal will keep much longer than the ground form known as laos powder.

Another rule in making curry pastes is to keep them as dry as possible. The first step of many curries is to fry the paste in oil or coconut cream, flavoring the oil with the spices, chiles, and other ingredients. If the paste is full of liquid, the mixture stews rather than fries, and the flavor infusion is not as thorough.

Mortar-and-pestle curry pastes generally do not need any added liquid, but if you are using a blender or food processor, you may have to add some liquid to chop the mixture thoroughly. If so, and if the paste is to be cooked in oil, use oil to thin it; if it is to be cooked in coconut milk, use the thick cream from the top of the milk (see page 38). In either case, you should then reduce or eliminate the oil or cream called for in the frying step and simply let the paste fry in its own fat.

An easier way to make curries is with packaged seasoning pastes. Many Asian markets carry a range of prepared curry pastes from Thailand in small cans or larger plastic tubs. One popular line includes the red, green, and Musaman types, for which recipes are given here, plus a relatively mild orange paste and a sour paste used mainly for seafood. Try these prepared pastes, but be careful—some of them are extremely hot. Start with less paste than is called for in the following recipes, and add more if necessary.

An even wider range of seasoning pastes is available from Indonesia, often by way of Holland. Name a traditional Indonesian dish, and there is probably a packaged seasoning mix or *bumbu* (also spelled *boemboe*) available for it. Because of the Dutch connection (see page 8), these mixes are often found in European-style delicatessens, along with the mustards and pickles.

Recipes for curry pastes begin on page 74; the step-by-step procedure in Preparing Curry Pastes, right, applies to all of the recipes. The quantities given for the pastes are sufficient for one large batch of curry, which can serve six to eight people as a main dish. The pastes keep for several weeks in a tightly closed jar in the refrigerator, so consider making extra for future dishes. With a prepared paste, a can or two of coconut milk, and some fish sauce on hand, you can whip up a tasty curry of meat, fish, poultry, or vegetables in as little as 15 minutes—less time than it takes to cook a pot of rice.

The curry pastes and similar seasoning mixtures so essential to many Southeast Asian dishes may be prepared in a mortar, a food processor, or a blender, but each approach requires a slightly different method. The photos in Preparing Curry Pastes, at right, show how to make the pastes using these various methods.

Step·by·Step

PREPARING CURRY PASTES

1. *An electric spice mill or a hand grinder does a quick job of grinding whole spices and dried chiles.*

2. *Hard dried ingredients such as lime peel and galangal may be soaked in warm water to soften.*

3. *To prepare in a mortar: Start with harder ingredients. Add kosher salt early to break down fibers. Finish with softer items such as fresh chiles. Add ground spices last.*

4. *To prepare in a food processor: Mince harder ingredients first by hand. Garlic and fresh chiles can be dropped in through the feed tube. Add remaining ingredients and process in pulses, stopping machine frequently to scrape down sides of work bowl. Add oil or thick coconut milk to facilitate blending.*

5. *To prepare in a blender: Use small accessory jar (which can double as a spice grinder) for blending small amounts. Mince all ingredients first; moisten with oil or coconut milk if necessary.*

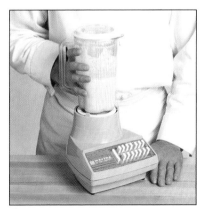

6. *If curry paste is to be cooked in coconut milk without frying first, use regular jar, adding more liquid.*

Curry pastes flavor curries as well as other savory dishes. Green pastes, based on fresh green chiles, are among the hottest. Red pastes may be more or less hot according to the type of chile used. Yellow pastes, with no chili and plenty of turmeric, are the mildest, but they are still full of garlic and other robust flavors.

GREEN CURRY PASTE
Krung kaeng keo wan
Thailand

This paste derives its name less from its color than from the fact that it is based on herbs and roots. Green curries are quite appropriate with poultry and seafood. This version is tame by Thai standards; for a hotter paste, include the seeds and veins of the chiles; for a breathtakingly hot paste, use tiny green Thai chiles.

> 3 slices fresh or dried galangal or 1 tablespoon dried krachai
> 2 strips Kaffir lime peel or 1 teaspoon lime zest
> 3 tablespoons minced coriander root
> 8 fresh serrano chiles or 5 jalapeños, seeds and veins removed

> 1 stalk lemongrass, minced
> 2 tablespoons minced garlic
> 2 tablespoons minced shallot or green onion
> 1 teaspoon shrimp paste
> 1 teaspoon ground coriander
> 2 to 3 tablespoons oil or coconut cream (see page 38), for blending (optional)

1. If using dried galangal or lime peel, soak in warm water until soft; drain and mince. Or grind in a spice grinder along with coriander root.

2. Combine all ingredients in a mortar or blender and pound to a paste, adding oil or coconut cream as necessary to facilitate blending. Cover and refrigerate until ready to use.

Makes ⅓ cup.

YELLOW CURRY PASTE
Thailand and Cambodia

Yellow curries are the mildest of all—they contain no chile. However, the quantity of garlic in this paste gives it a special pungency of its own.

- 2 stalks lemongrass, thinly sliced
- 1 head garlic, separated into cloves and peeled
- 1 teaspoon kosher salt
- 3 slices fresh galangal, minced
- 8 strips Kaffir lime peel, soaked until soft, drained, and minced
- ½ teaspoon turmeric

Combine ingredients in a mortar or blender and pound or blend to a paste. Cover and refrigerate until ready to use.

Makes ⅓ cup.

RED CURRY PASTE I
Krung kaeng ped
Thailand

This is a fairly hot paste based on the small dried *serrano* chile. Remove the seeds or include them according to taste. If you are using dried Thai chiles, you will probably want to remove the seeds.

- 7 small dried serrano chiles, finely chopped
- 1 stalk lemongrass, thinly sliced
- 2 tablespoons minced garlic
- ¼ cup minced shallot or onion
- 1 tablespoon minced coriander root
- 2 slices fresh galangal, minced or 2 slices dried galangal or 2 teaspoons dried krachai, soaked, drained, and minced
- 3 strips Kaffir lime peel, soaked, drained, and minced
- 1 teaspoon kosher salt
- 1 teaspoon shrimp paste
- 2 teaspoons ground coriander
- ½ teaspoon ground caraway or cumin

Combine ingredients in a mortar or blender and pound or blend to a paste. Store covered in the refrigerator until ready to use.

Makes ⅓ cup.

RED CURRY PASTE II
Cambodia

Cambodian red curry paste is not as hot as its Thai counterpart, but it should still taste of red chiles. The relatively mild, long red California or New Mexico chile is ideal for this purpose.

- 2 dried California or New Mexico chiles
- 2 stalks lemongrass, thinly sliced
- 1 head garlic, separated into cloves and peeled
- 3 slices fresh galangal, minced
- 8 strips Kaffir lime peel, soaked, drained, and minced
- 1 teaspoon kosher salt
- 1 teaspoon shrimp paste
- 1 teaspoon ground coriander
- ½ teaspoon ground cumin

1. Split chiles down the side and remove seeds and veins. Tear flesh into small pieces and soak in warm water until soft. Drain.

2. Combine chiles, lemongrass, garlic, galangal, lime peel, salt, and shrimp paste in a mortar and pound to a paste. Add ground spices and combine. Cover and refrigerate until ready to use.

Makes ⅓ cup.

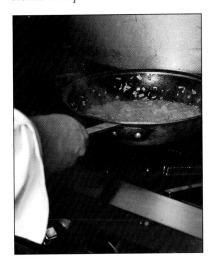

MUSAMAN CURRY PASTE
Krung kaeng musaman
Thailand

This cooked curry paste, a relatively late addition to the Thai repertoire, uses many of the spices common to northern Indian cooking. The name "Musaman" is a corruption of "Moslem."

- 1 tablespoon coriander seed
- 5 cloves or ¼ teaspoon ground cloves
- 1 cinnamon stick (1 in. piece) or ½ teaspoon ground cinnamon
  Seeds from 5 cardamom pods (a generous ¼ teaspoon)
- 1 teaspoon cumin seed
- ½ teaspoon fennel or anise seed
- 12 black peppercorns or ½ teaspoon freshly ground pepper
- 7 small dried chiles, seeds removed
- 1 tablespoon oil
- 2 tablespoons minced garlic
- ¼ cup minced shallot or onion
- 1 tablespoon minced fresh galangal or 2 slices dried
- ½ teaspoon shrimp paste
- 1 teaspoon kosher salt

1. If using whole spices combine coriander, cloves, cinnamon, cardamom, cumin, fennel, peppercorns, and dried galangal (if used) in a small dry skillet and toast until quite fragrant but not too brown. Add chiles, toast a few seconds more, and transfer contents to spice grinder. Grind to a powder.

2. Heat oil in skillet over low heat and cook garlic, shallot, and fresh galangal (if used) until they begin to soften. Add shrimp paste and cook another few minutes, until strong smell dissipates. Be careful not to let the mixture burn. Allow to cool, transfer to mortar or blender, add salt, and grind to a smooth paste. Add ground spice mixture and blend thoroughly. Store in a covered jar in refrigerator until ready to use.

Makes ⅓ cup.

1. Combine *prahok* and fish sauce in a small bowl and mash with a fork. Remove any bones. Set aside.

2. In a skillet bring coconut milk to a boil. Add curry paste and cook over high heat until reduced by half. Add pork and cook until meat is nearly done. Add onion, sugar, and prahok mixture and cook until thick (about 3 minutes). Transfer to a serving bowl. Serve with green onion and raw vegetable garnish to dip in the curry sauce.

Serves 3 to 4 with other dishes.

<u>Note</u> Prahok is a salty condiment of fermented gouramy fish—a sort of solid version of fish sauce. It is available in Southeast Asian groceries in small jars from Thailand, labeled pickled gouramy fish or with the Vietnamese name *mam ca sac*. Philippine *bagoong* is more or less equivalent. If unavailable, rinsed and mashed anchovies are an acceptable substitute.

"MOSLEM-STYLE" CURRY
Kaeng musaman
Thailand

As the name implies, this curry is derived from the cuisine of the Moslem world, especially that of northern India. The fish sauce, however, is a typically Thai touch. This curry works equally well with lamb or kid, although neither meat is especially popular in Thailand.

> 1 pound beef chuck, in ½-inch cubes, or 2 pounds chicken parts, cut into braising pieces (see page 19)
> ½ cup roasted peanuts
> 1½ cups thin coconut milk (see page 38)
> 1 cup diced potato or sweet potato
> ½ cup thick coconut milk
> 3 tablespoons Musaman Curry Paste (see page 75)
> 2 tablespoons Tamarind Water (see page 34) or lime juice
> 1 teaspoon brown or palm sugar
> 2 tablespoons fish sauce

Instead of stewing cubes, this unusual Cambodian pork curry is made with quick-cooking minced or ground meat. The whole dish, with its raw vegetable garnish, can be put together in the time it takes to cook the rice.

YELLOW CURRIED PORK
Cambodia

Dipping an assortment of raw vegetables in a curry sauce provides them with another dimension of flavor and texture.

> ½ teaspoon prahok (fish paste— see Note), mashed
> 2 teaspoons fish sauce
> ¼ cup medium coconut milk (see page 38)
> 1 tablespoon Yellow Curry Paste (see page 75)
> ½ cup ground pork
> ¼ cup diced yellow onion
> ½ teaspoon sugar
> 2 tablespoons minced green onion, for garnish
> Vegetable garnish: cucumber slices, sliced cabbage, bean sprouts, Thai eggplant, mint sprigs, red chile

1. In a saucepan simmer beef and peanuts in thin coconut milk until tender, about 30 minutes. Add potato for last 15 minutes of cooking.

2. In a wok or deep skillet, heat thick coconut milk over medium heat until slightly reduced. Add curry paste and cook until fragrant. Add meat and potato mixture with its liquid, stir in Tamarind Water, sugar, and fish sauce, and simmer until mixture is slightly thickened (about 5 minutes).

Serves 4 to 6 with other dishes.

GREEN CURRIED SHRIMP
Kaeng keo wan kung
Thailand

In Thailand, shrimp are abundant in both fresh and salt water, so they are widely used. But feel free to substitute other seafoods, depending on what is locally available and in season: mussels, clams, squid, crab, lobster, crayfish tails, or cubes of mild-flavored fish. If using cooked seafood, add it at the end, just long enough to reheat.

   2 *cups (14 oz can) thick coconut milk (see page 38)*
   ¼ *cup coconut cream, skimmed from the coconut milk*
   2 *tablespoons Green Curry Paste (see page 74)*
   1 *cup diced new potatoes*
   1 *pound shrimp, peeled and deveined*
   ½ *cup water*
   3 *Kaffir lime leaves (optional)*
   2 *teaspoons fish sauce, or to taste*
   1 *cup peeled, seeded, and roughly chopped tomatoes*
   ½ *cup fresh coriander*

Spoon coconut cream into a wok or large skillet (use a little less if some was used in grinding curry paste). Add curry paste, bring to a boil, and cook until oil begins to separate. Reduce heat to medium and add potatoes. Cook, stirring, until potatoes are nearly done. Add shrimp, coconut milk, water, and lime leaves (if used). Bring to a boil and cook until shrimp and potatoes are done. If sauce thickens too quickly, thin with a little more water. Season to taste with fish sauce and stir in tomatoes and coriander.

Serves 4 with other dishes.

A Thai green curry, such as this one made with shrimp, is incomplete without fresh herbs—basil, mint, or, in this case, fresh coriander.

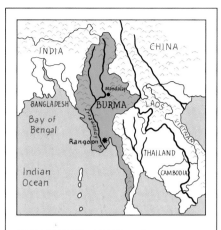

BURMESE CUISINE

To Westerners the cuisine of Burma is one of the least known of Southeast Asia, in part because that country is not a popular tourist destination. Geographically, Burma lies between Thailand and India, and it is perhaps easiest to describe its cuisine by comparison with that of its neighbors. In general, Burmese food has much in common with Thai and Malay food, but shows more Indian influence.

A Burmese curry, for example, is less intricately spiced than its Indian counterpart; still, the same basic spices are featured—notably turmeric, coriander, and cumin. Legumes such as split peas and lentils are also widely used, another sign of Indian influence. Burmese cooking uses both fresh and dried chiles more sparingly than does Thai cooking. Yet a Thai cook would feel quite at home with the coconut milk, ginger, dried shrimp, shrimp paste, and fish sauce used in many Burmese dishes.

Burmese cooking shares another trait with the other cuisines of Southeast Asia, which sets all of them apart from Indian and Chinese cooking—a love of crisp raw vegetables, either in salads or as an accompaniment to cooked dishes. Garlic is indispensible in Burmese cooking, particularly in the form of garlic-flavored oil. Slowly frying sliced or minced garlic until crisp thoroughly infuses the oil with garlic flavor. Garlic oil is used in both salads and cooked dishes, with the fried flakes often serving as garnish.

BURMESE DRY PORK CURRY
Burma

This is a dry curry in the sense that it is cooked until little liquid remains. The oil naturally separates when the sauce is sufficiently reduced. The seasonings show a strong Indian influence typical of Burmese curries.

The versatile spice blend Garam Masala is sold in Indian markets and some spice shops. You can also make your own by toasting and grinding the whole spices. Recipes vary, but the blend given below is typical. Don't make more than you expect to use in a month or so, since the spices will lose flavor after grinding.

> 2 tablespoons minced garlic
> 1 tablespoon minced ginger
> 2 teaspoons minced fresh turmeric or ½ teaspoon ground
> 1 teaspoon kosher salt
> 2 tablespoons oil
> 1 cup sliced onion
> 1 teaspoon, or to taste, Garam Masala (see below)
> 1 teaspoon ground mild chile or hot paprika
> 1 pound pork shoulder, in 1-inch cubes
> 1 pound boiling potatoes, diced
> 2 cups thin coconut milk (see page 38)
> 2 tablespoons fish sauce

Garam Masala

> ½ teaspoon each cumin seed, coriander seed, and crumbled cinnamon stick
> 1 teaspoon black peppercorns
> 3 cloves
> Seeds from 4 cardamom pods (about ¼ teaspoon)

1. *To prepare in a mortar:* Pound garlic, ginger, and turmeric to a paste with salt; set aside. *To prepare by hand:* Mince the fresh ingredients together as finely as possible and combine with salt.

2. In a wok or skillet, heat oil over medium-low heat. Add onion, paste, Garam Masala, and ground chile and cook slowly, stirring to prevent scorching, until onions are translu-cent and liquid is nearly evaporated (oil will separate). Add pork cubes and brown lightly on all sides. Add potatoes, coconut milk, and fish sauce. Bring to a boil, reduce heat, and simmer until liquid is reduced to less than ½ cup. While sauce is reducing, taste for seasoning and adjust if necessary. If more Garam Masala is needed, cook at least 5 minutes after adding it.

Serves 4 to 6 with other dishes.

Garam Masala In a small dry skillet, toast spices over medium heat until slightly darkened and quite fragrant. Shake or stir constantly to prevent scorching. Grind them to a powder in a spice grinder or mortar. Store in a tightly covered jar.

Makes about 1 tablespoon.

Variation Beef, chicken, or shrimp may be substituted for the pork, although the cooking times will vary. Beef cubes or chicken with bones will take slightly longer to cook; thinly sliced beef, boneless chicken, or shrimp will cook quickly and should be added after the potatoes are done and the sauce is already thickened.

GREEN DUCK CURRY
Kaeng keo wan ped
Thailand

Southeast Asian ducks are smaller and leaner than our domestic ducks, so they are cooked more or less the same way as chicken. The preliminary browning in step 2 of this recipe is a technique borrowed from the Chinese to rid a typical American duck of much of its excess fat. This curry will improve with a day or more of aging in the refrigerator before serving; chilling also makes it easier to remove the excess fat from the sauce.

1 duckling with giblets, 4 to 5 pounds, cleaned inside and out and disjointed
  Kosher salt

2 cups each *thick and thin coconut milk (see page 38)*

¼ cup coconut cream, skimmed from the thick coconut milk

2½ tablespoons Green Curry Paste (see page 74)

4 Kaffir lime leaves

¼ cup seeded and sliced fresh chiles
  Fish sauce, to taste

½ cup fresh basil, mint, or coriander leaves

1. Remove head and feet of duck, if present, and save for stock. Set aside liver for another use. Dry duck thoroughly with paper towels. Sprinkle skin side generously with salt and set aside 15 minutes.

2. Brush off salt and chop duck into braising pieces. Heat a large skillet or wok over medium-high heat. Add a few duck pieces and brown thoroughly. Keep heat as high as possible without burning rendered fat. Drain on paper towels and continue browning a few pieces at a time. Discard rendered fat and wipe pan clean.

3. Turn heat to medium. Spoon coconut cream into pan. When bubbling, add curry paste and lime leaves and cook, stirring constantly, until oil begins to separate. Add duck pieces and toss to season evenly with paste. Cook another 5 minutes, being careful not to let paste scorch.

4. Add thick and thin coconut milk, bring just to a boil, and reduce heat as low as possible. Simmer until duck is tender, about 1 hour and 15 minutes. Proceed to next step or, for better results, transfer curry to a bowl and refrigerate covered overnight or for up to 3 days.

5. Skim off excess fat from curry and add chiles. Season to taste with fish sauce and simmer 5 minutes more. Stir in fresh herbs and serve. There should be plenty of thin sauce.

Serves 4 to 6 with other dishes.

Burmese curries such as this version made of pork are often cooked "dry," that is, until the sauce reduces to a clinging consistency and the oil begins to separate.

FISH CURRY WITH COCONUT MILK

This quick, easy curry, native to no particular country but evoking the typical flavors of the whole region, can be made with any mild white-fleshed fish—snapper, ocean perch, rockfish, catfish, or flounder, to name just a few.

> 1 tablespoon each *minced fresh lemongrass, ginger, and garlic*
> Pinch of kosher salt
> 1 teaspoon dried krachai
> ½ teaspoon coriander seed
> Seeds from 2 cardamom pods (about ⅛ teaspoon)
> 1 small dried chile, seeds and veins removed
> 2 tablespoons oil
> 2 green onions, sliced
> 3 tablespoons fish sauce
> 2 cups (14 oz can) thick coconut milk (see page 38)
> 1 to 1½ pounds mild white fish fillets, in 1-inch cubes
> Fresh coriander or mint, for garnish (optional)

1. *To prepare in a mortar:* Pound lemongrass, ginger, and garlic to a paste with a pinch of salt. *To prepare in a blender:* Chop them together in a 1-cup blender jar.

2. Combine krachai, coriander, cardamom, and chile in a spice grinder and grind finely. Add to ingredients in mortar or blender and grind to a smooth paste.

3. Heat oil in a wok or saucepan over medium-high heat. Add green onions and curry paste and cook, stirring to break up the paste, until very fragrant, about 3 minutes. Add fish sauce and coconut milk, bring almost to a boil, and add fish pieces. Bring back to boil, reduce to a simmer, and cook until fish is done, about 6 minutes. Taste sauce and correct seasoning, if necessary. Serve over rice, garnished with coriander or mint leaves, if desired.

Serves 4 with other dishes.

VEGETABLE CURRY WITH COCONUT MILK
Sayur lodeh
Indonesia and Malaysia

Sayur is a variable category of vegetable dishes cooked in coconut milk. Some are thin and eaten as soups, and others, like the following version, are thicker and are served over rice. Using a prepared curry paste (Bumbu Sayur Lodeh, see page 73) in place of the curry paste, ginger, and turmeric makes this a quick and easy side dish to complement *satés* or other dry-cooked dishes.

> 2 cups (14 oz can) thick coconut milk (see page 38)
> 2 tablespoons coconut cream, skimmed from the coconut milk
> 1 to 2 teaspoons green or red curry paste (see pages 74–75)
> 1 teaspoon minced ginger
> 1 medium onion, diced
> ½ teaspoon turmeric
> ¼ cup Tamarind Water (see page 34)
> Salt or fish sauce, to taste
> 2 cups assorted vegetables: cauliflower or broccoli florets; sweet potatoes, peeled and diced; green beans, trimmed and cut in 2-inch lengths; red bell peppers, sliced; zucchini, sliced; cabbage, cut into 1-inch squares

1. Heat coconut cream in a wok or saucepan over medium heat. Stir in curry paste, ginger, onion, and turmeric; cook until fragrant. Add Tamarind Water and coconut milk, bring to a boil, and reduce to a simmer. Season to taste with salt or fish sauce. The recipe can be prepared to this point and removed from heat up to an hour ahead.

2. Arrange vegetables in order of cooking time. Cauliflower, broccoli, and sweet potato will take about 10 minutes, green beans and bell peppers about 5 minutes, zucchini and cabbage just long enough to heat through, 1 or 2 minutes. Add the longest-cooking vegetables first, finishing with the fastest cooking. Adjust heat to keep liquid at a lively simmer. Check seasoning and serve.

Serves 4 to 6 with other dishes.

CHICKEN BRAISED IN COCONUT MILK
Opor ayam
Indonesia

This dish could just as well be labeled a soup as a curry, because it includes a lot of flavored liquid.

> 1 chicken (3 to 4 lb), disjointed
> 2 tablespoons Tamarind Water (see page 34) or lemon juice
> Kosher salt and freshly ground pepper
> ½ teaspoon black peppercorns
> 1 tablespoon ground coriander
> ½ teaspoon ground cumin
> ½ cup minced onion or shallot
> 3 cloves garlic
> 2 tablespoons minced ginger
> 4 macadamia nuts
> Pinch sugar
> 1 tablespoon oil
> 1 salam leaf or 2 curry leaves
> 2 cups medium coconut milk (see page 38)
> Coconut cream, skimmed from the medium coconut milk (optional)

1. Sprinkle chicken pieces with Tamarind Water, pinch of salt, and pepper and let stand 30 minutes, turning occasionally to marinate evenly. Meanwhile, prepare seasoning paste.

2. *To prepare in a mortar:* Grind together peppercorns, coriander, and cumin. Add onion, garlic, ginger, macadamia nuts, ½ teaspoon salt, and sugar and grind to a smooth paste. *To prepare in a blender or food processor:* Use ground peppercorns and spices. Add coconut cream as necessary to facilitate blending.

3. Heat oil in a wok or deep skillet over medium heat. Drain chicken pieces and brown a few at a time, removing them from the pan as they are browned. Add paste and salam leaf to pan and cook until fragrant, stirring constantly. Add coconut milk, return chicken to pan, and simmer until chicken is tender, 25 to 30 minutes. Taste for seasoning and adjust if necessary. Serve hot or lukewarm.

Serves 6 to 8 with other dishes.

BEEF CURRY, SUMATRA STYLE
Kalio
Malaysia and Indonesia

This rich, full-flavored curry is typical of the Malay Peninsula and the island of Sumatra, which face each other across the Strait of Malacca. Adjust the amount of red chile according to taste and the strength of the chiles.

Thailand has its own version of this dish, *Panang nuea,* named after the Malaysian city of Penang (see variation below). Although the ingredients are similar, the technique is quite different.

Rendang simply takes this dish one step further (see variation below), cooking it until the liquid is evaporated and the meat begins to fry in the rendered coconut oil.

> 2 tablespoons chopped fresh red chile or 4 teaspoons sambal ulek
> 3 or 4 slices ginger
> 2 slices fresh galangal or ½ teaspoon ground
> 3 cloves garlic
> ½ cup chopped onion
> 1 teaspoon kosher salt
> ¼ teaspoon ground turmeric
> 2 teaspoons ground coriander
> 1 cup each thick and thin coconut milk (see page 38)
> 1 stalk lemongrass, cut into 2-inch lengths and bruised
> 1 salam leaf or curry leaf
> 1½ pounds stewing beef (chuck or similar cut), in 2-inch cubes

1. In a blender, food processor, or mortar, blend chile, ginger, galangal, garlic, onion, salt, turmeric, and coriander to a paste, adding thick coconut milk as needed to facilitate blending.

2. In a wok, deep skillet, or heavy saucepan, combine paste, remaining thick and thin coconut milk, lemongrass, salam leaf, and beef. Bring mixture just to a boil, reduce heat, and simmer uncovered, stirring frequently, until beef is tender and sauce is somewhat thickened (about 2 to 3 hours). Taste for seasoning and adjust as necessary.

Serves 6 to 8 with other dishes.

Beef Curry, Penang Style (*Panang nuea*) Cut the beef into thin rectangular slices, as for stir-frying. Use Red Curry Paste I (see page 75) in place of the paste in step 1. Boil the thick coconut milk down until reduced by half, add the curry paste and other seasonings plus 2 tablespoons fish sauce, and simmer 10 minutes. Add the thin coconut milk, reduce again until thick, and add the sliced beef. Simmer just until beef is cooked (3 to 5 minutes).

Dry Beef Curry (*Rendang*) Prepare ingredients for Beef Curry, Sumatra Style as directed above, then continue cooking over medium heat, stirring frequently, until liquid evaporates and oil begins to separate. Take care at this point that the mixture does not burn; it should be nicely browned but not scorched.

Rich curries, thick with reduced coconut milk, are favorites in the outer islands of Indonesia and the western part of Malaysia. This Sumatran version with beef is a typical curry of the region.

PHILIPPINE CUISINE

Modern Philippine cooking, like the Filipinos themselves, combines Malay, Chinese, and Western elements. Ethnically related to the Malay and Polynesian peoples, the indigenous people of the islands absorbed influences from Chinese traders, Moslem missionaries, and European adventurers. Three-and-a-half centuries of Spanish rule and a half century of American occupation left an indelible Western stamp on Philippine culture, ethnic makeup, and cuisine.

Ingredients in common with Malay and mainland cuisines include rice, coconuts and their milk, fish sauce, fermented fish and shrimp pastes, and tamarind. A pan-Pacific favorite, raw fish marinated in lime juice with coconut milk, is virtually the same as the Tahitian version, but goes by the Spanish name *ceviche*. The Chinese introduced soy sauce, noodles, and dough-wrapped foods. The Spanish brought olive oil, tomatoes, and spicy *chorizo* (sausages), as well as introducing many culinary terms to the language. The name of the noodle dish *Pancit Bihon Guisado* (see page 109) illustrates all these varied influences: *pancit bihon* is the Philippine derivative of a Chinese name for a certain type of noodle; *guisado* is the Spanish word for sautéed.

A distinctive feature of Philippine cuisine is the way cooks blend many flavors, particularly sour, salty, and peppery. Garlic slowly cooked in oil forms the basis of most savory dishes, including the famous *adobo*.

ADOBOS

The Phillipine adobo, like the curries of other countries, probably originated as a way to preserve meat. In this case, the preserving agent is not chile or other spices, but vinegar. Adobos may be served with or without a lot of sauce, as the following two versions illustrate, but the tastes of vinegar and garlic should always predominate. Palm vinegar, a mild, greenish vinegar made from palm sap and sold in Philippine markets, gives the most authentic flavor to adobos; however, Japanese-style rice vinegar will do.

PORK ADOBO
Adobong baboy
Philippines

In this version of adobo, cubes of pork are boiled in a vinegar and garlic mixture until the liquid evaporates and they begin to fry in their own rendered fat. Use pork with some visible fat, either from the shoulder or the nearby section of the loin (usually sold as "country-style spareribs").

- 1½ *pounds boneless pork, in 1-inch cubes*
- ½ *cup rice or palm vinegar*
- 6 *cloves garlic, minced*
- 3 *tablespoons soy sauce or fish sauce*
- ¼ *teaspoon freshly ground pepper*
- 1½ *cups water*
- 1 *bay leaf*

1. In a bowl, combine pork cubes, vinegar, garlic, soy sauce, and pepper and marinate 1 to 3 hours in the refrigerator.

2. Transfer all to a nonaluminum saucepan, add 1 cup of the water and bay leaf, and bring to a boil uncovered. Adjust heat so meat cooks at a lively simmer but does not boil too rapidly.

3. Cook until liquid is nearly gone, then reduce heat further. Mixture will sizzle and pop as the last bits of water evaporate, then the pork cubes will begin to brown in the remaining fat. Turn cubes to brown evenly and remove from heat if mixture shows signs of scorching.

4. Remove pork cubes to serving dish. Add ½ cup of the water to pan and bring to a boil, stirring to scrape up browned bits from pan. Pour over pork. Serve with rice.

Serves 4 with other dishes.

Variation Use a mixture of boneless pork and chicken, cut with bones into braising pieces (see page 19). Cook only until liquid is reduced to ½ cup, then brown meats in a separate pan as in Chicken Adobo With Coconut Milk (see page 83).

POT ROAST, PHILIPPINE STYLE
Mechado
Philippines

This is not an adobo, but a touch of vinegar gives this tender braised beef dish an unmistakably Philippine flavor. The name comes from the Spanish *mecha,* which means both wick and strip of bacon; because Philippine beef is usually lean, it is larded with bacon to baste it internally while cooking. American beef has enough fat to make this treatment unnecessary.

- 2 *tablespoons oil or bacon drippings*
- 1 *beef pot roast (2 to 3 lb in one piece): cross-rib, chuck, or round*
  Freshly ground pepper, to taste
- 4 *cups water*
- ¼ *cup rice or palm vinegar*
- 3 *tablespoons soy sauce*
- 1 *cup fresh or canned peeled tomatoes, chopped*
- 4 *cloves garlic, whole*
- 1 *pound boiling onions, peeled*
- 1 *pound potatoes, cut into 1½-inch cubes*
- 2 *carrots, cut into 1-inch lengths*
  Salt and freshly ground pepper, to taste

1. Heat oil in a skillet or heavy-bottomed casserole. Season beef with pepper and brown on all sides. Transfer meat to a large saucepan, or drain off oil from casserole. Add water, vinegar, soy sauce, tomatoes, and garlic. Cover pot, and simmer until meat is tender (2 to 3 hours).

2. When meat is nearly done, add onions, potatoes, and carrots and continue cooking until vegetables are done. Remove beef and vegetables, slice beef, and arrange all on a platter. Boil down sauce until reduced by one third, correct seasoning, and pour over meat. Leftovers are good reheated in sauce.

Serves 6 to 8 with other dishes.

CHICKEN ADOBO WITH COCONUT MILK
Adobong manok sa gata
Philippines

  1 *small frying chicken* or *2 to 3 pounds chicken parts*
  ¾ *cup* each *water and rice or palm vinegar*
  1½ *cups thin coconut milk (see Note, and page 38)*
  6 *cloves garlic, minced*
  ½ *teaspoon kosher salt*
  1 *teaspoon black peppercorns, cracked*
  1 *teaspoon annatto seeds (optional)*
  2 *bay leaves*
  1 *to 2 tablespoons oil, if needed
      Fish sauce, to taste
      Freshly ground pepper, to taste*
  2 *tablespoons coconut cream (see Note)*

1. Disjoint chicken and place in a nonaluminum saucepan. Add water, vinegar, coconut milk, garlic, salt, peppercorns, annatto (if used), and bay leaves. Marinate 30 minutes to 1 hour, then bring to a boil. Reduce heat and simmer until chicken is tender, 30 to 45 minutes.

2. Remove from heat, remove chicken from sauce, and let sauce stand a few minutes until fat rises to surface. The recipe may be prepared to this point several hours to several days ahead; refrigerate, covered, if storing longer than 2 hours.

3. Skim fat from sauce and place in a skillet. Add oil if necessary to cover bottom of skillet. Heat fat over medium-high heat and brown chicken pieces well. Meanwhile, bring sauce to a boil and reduce by two thirds. Season sauce to taste with fish sauce and additional pepper, if needed.

4. Transfer browned chicken pieces to a warm platter. Stir coconut cream into sauce and pour over chicken.

Serves 4 with other dishes.

<u>Note</u> If using canned coconut milk in step 1, spoon off the cream and reserve for step 4, and add enough water to make 1½ cups. If using homemade coconut milk, skim coconut cream from first pressing, and use the milk from the second pressing.

Variation In step 3, chicken may be broiled or grilled rather than cooked in oil.

Philippine adobos may be thin or, as in this version, thickened with coconut milk. The brick red annatto seeds, which give the sauce a subtle flavor and a warm yellow color, are not intended to be eaten.

A THAI DINNER FOR SIX

Meatballs Wrapped in Noodles
(see page 47)

Cucumber Salad
(see page 113)

Dancing Prawns

Green Chicken Curry

Sour Fish Soup
(see page 65)

Rice

Fresh fruit

Thai Iced Tea
(see page 20)

A variety of colors, flavors, aromas, and textures is the key to an elegant Thai meal. This menu combines hotter and milder flavors, crunchy and soft textures, and exotic aromas around a dramatic centerpiece of "dancing" grilled shrimp. All the recipes in this menu serve six.

DANCING PRAWNS

This attractive presentation works best with good-sized shrimp such as the Southeast Asian "tiger prawns." In Thailand, the shrimp would be grilled with the heads on, but you may remove them if you wish.

> 1 tablespoon minced garlic
> 2 tablespoons minced shallot
> 1 teaspoon minced fresh galangal or ginger
> 2 teaspoons minced lemongrass Pinch salt
> 1 tablespoon each lemon juice and soy sauce
> 2 tablespoons Chinese rice wine or dry sherry
> Large shrimp or freshwater prawns, preferably with heads on, 2 or 3 per person
> ½ orange or apple Coriander sprigs, for garnish Lime wedges, for garnish

1. In a mortar, pound garlic, shallot, galangal, and lemongrass to a paste with salt. Transfer to a shallow bowl and stir in lemon juice, soy sauce, and wine.

2. With a small knife or scissors, split shrimp shells down the back, but leave attached. (If heads are present, carefully separate shell where tail joins head, then split tail shell open.) Devein. Toss in marinade and let stand 30 minutes to 3 hours.

3. Soak bamboo skewers in water 30 minutes and drain. Thread each shrimp lengthwise on a skewer, starting at tail end and coming out through head, if present. Push skewer on through until pointed end extends 3 inches beyond shrimp. Handling by pointed ends, grill until meat is opaque. To serve, place orange half cut side down on plate and insert pointed ends of skewers. Garnish with coriander sprigs and lime wedges.

Variation Dancing Prawns may be broiled instead of grilled. Position exposed part of skewers away from fire or wrap in foil to prevent burning.

GREEN CHICKEN CURRY
Kaeng keo wan kai

This souplike curry will improve with a day or more of aging in the refrigerator before serving. Chilling also makes it easier to remove the excess fat from the sauce.

> 1 large frying chicken, (4 to 5 lb), cleaned inside and out and disjointed
> 2 cups each thick and thin coconut milk (see page 38)
> ¼ cup coconut cream, skimmed from the thick coconut milk
> 2½ tablespoons Green Curry Paste (see page 74)
> 4 Kaffir lime leaves
> ¼ cup seeded and sliced chiles Fish sauce, to taste
> ½ cup fresh basil, mint, or coriander

1. Remove head and feet of chicken, if present, and save for stock. Set aside liver for another use. Remove and discard kidneys and excess fat. Rinse chicken, dry thoroughly with paper towels, and chop into braising pieces (see page 19).

2. Place coconut cream in a wok or deep skillet over medium heat. When bubbly, add curry paste and lime leaves and cook, stirring constantly, until oil begins to separate from cream. Add chicken pieces and toss to season evenly with paste. Cook another 5 minutes, being careful not to let paste scorch.

3. Add thick and thin coconut milk, bring just to a boil, and reduce heat as low as possible. Simmer until chicken is tender, about 1 hour. Recipe may be prepared to this point 1 to 3 days ahead and refrigerated.

4. Skim off excess fat from curry and add chiles. Season to taste with fish sauce and simmer 5 minutes more. Stir in fresh herbs and serve. There should be plenty of thin sauce.

A study in contrasting flavors and textures, this elegant Thai meal combines rich curry, sour seafood soup, simply seasoned grilled shrimp, and fresh fruit.

Pounded fresh ingredients such as lemongrass and ginger flavor many Southeast Asian dishes, including most of the grilled foods in this chapter.

Grilling

G rilling foods directly over a wood
or charcoal fire is one of the most
ancient of cooking methods, and it
remains one of the most popular. Each
country of Southeast Asia has its favorite
grilled foods, including the skewered
and grilled meats known as *saté*, succulent,
aromatic barbecued chicken (see
the Vietnamese version on page 93), and fish
grilled in banana-leaf wrappers (see
the Indonesian Outdoor Buffet menu on page
96). A particularly interesting dish is the
special stuffed chicken on page 94, which is
flavored Asian style but roasted Western style.

GRILLING

Grilling, or barbecuing, as it is often known, means cooking food directly over an open fire, usually supported by a metal grill. In the traditional Southeast Asian kitchen, the fire is the same one used to cook foods in pots and pans; one simply places a grill on top of the same open-topped clay brazier that serves as a stove.

Modern cooks generally use a separate grill, often similar to a Japanese hibachi. Most of these grills are small compared to a typical American barbecue. The reason is mainly economic: Large fires use a lot of fuel. When foods are cut in smaller pieces they cook more quickly, using a minimum of fuel. Most of the recipes in this book can be prepared on a single- or double-burner hibachi. If you are preparing a number of grilled dishes, as in the Indonesian Outdoor Buffet menu on page 96, a larger grill is in order.

Many cooks prefer to use lumps of natural hardwood charcoal, such as Mexican mesquite, rather than manufactured briquets. Whichever you use, be sure the charcoal is completely lit; charcoal that is still catching fire can give an unpleasantly smoky, tarlike flavor to the food.

In the following recipes, a medium-hot fire is one in which the coals are still glowing red, but beginning to form a layer of gray ash. You should be able to hold your hand comfortably a few inches above the grill for no more than 4 or 5 seconds. A moderate fire is cooler, registering 8 to 10 seconds by the same test. You can regulate the heat by pushing the coals together or spreading them out.

When you are eating outdoors you may place a hibachi on the table, either for do-it-yourself cooking or just so the cook does not have to keep getting up to tend the fire. For indoor tabletop cooking, various small gas-fired and electric grills are available. When using a tabletop grill, be sure to protect the table with a heatproof pad or trivet.

Caution Never use a charcoal grill indoors without adequate ventilation; charcoal fires produce carbon monoxide gas, which can quickly concentrate to poisonous levels in an enclosed space.

Very few special tools are needed for Asian-style grilling. Thin bamboo skewers are ideal for _satés;_ soaking them in water for 30 minutes before skewering the food helps prevent them from burning. Satés can sometimes be handled by their skewers, but a pair of tongs is useful for turning other foods on the grill. A brush is handy for basting with marinades. Any of the following grilled recipes can be prepared under a gas or electric broiler.

Western-style ovens are no more common in Southeast Asia than broilers, so roasting is not a common home-cooking technique. The few roasted meats that are sold are generally cooked commercially in restaurants and takeout food shops in the cities. However, a few countries have developed roasted specialties; the Philippine boned and stuffed chicken on page 94 is an example.

Another form of roasting is cooking foods in the ashes of the cooking fire. The Laotian raw beef salad on page 94 is adapted from this technique.

SATÉ

The small pieces of skewered meats known as _saté_ are the best-known form of Southeast Asian grilled foods. The name, also spelled _satay,_ comes from Malay, and is probably derived from the English word "steak." Among Moslem Malays and Indonesians, the meats are typically beef, lamb, chicken, or shrimp, but the style of the dish has traveled widely, and non-Moslems enjoy pork as well.

Because the most typical forms of saté are served with a spicy peanut sauce, some people assume that saté is a flavor, like curry (an equally erroneous notion—see page 72). In fact, all it means is "skewered and grilled." _Saté manis,_ "sweet saté," has a marinade based on sweet soy sauce (kecap manis); _saté bumbu,_ "spiced saté," features meat that is partially cooked and marinated in a highly spiced sauce; and there are numerous other variations of skewered, grilled foods.

If charcoal grilling is impractical, you can still make a passable version of saté under the broiler, in a skillet with a ridged surface, or even on a lightly oiled griddle.

BASIC SATÉ WITH PEANUT SAUCE
Indonesia and Malaysia

In this, the simplest form of _saté,_ the meat or poultry is only lightly seasoned by the marinade, so its own flavors can come through to meet those of the sauce. Try it with chicken, beef, lamb, pork, or even turkey leg meat—the last is not authentic, but it is delicious.

- ½ to ¾ pound boneless meat or poultry
- 2 cloves garlic
- ¼ teaspoon kosher salt
- ¼ teaspoon ground coriander
  Pinch sugar
- 2 tablespoons Tamarind Water (see page 34)
  Peanut Sauce I (see page 36), for accompaniment

1. If using poultry, cut into ½-inch cubes or strips up to 2 inches long. Beef, lamb, or pork may be cut into similar cubes. Or, for faster cooking, slice thinly across the grain and cut the slices into 1-inch squares.

2. _To prepare in a mortar:_ Pound garlic and salt to a paste. _To prepare by hand:_ Mince garlic as finely as possible, then sprinkle with salt and mash with the side of a knife blade. Transfer garlic paste to a bowl, add coriander, sugar, and Tamarind Water, and stir to dissolve. Marinate meat in tamarind mixture 30 minutes to 1 hour.

3. Thread meat on ends of skewers, 2 or 3 pieces per skewer. If using long strips or thin slices of meat, stretch them out to equal thickness for even cooking. Grill over a medium-hot charcoal fire until meat is firm and springy, basting once with any remaining marinade. Serve with Peanut Sauce I.

Serves 4 with other dishes.

PORK SATÉ MARINATED IN COCONUT MILK
Thailand

These skewers of thinly sliced pork cook very quickly, making this an ideal *saté* for tabletop cooking. Strips of chicken breast may be substituted for the pork.

- ⅓ *cup medium or thick coconut milk (see page 38)*
- 1 *teaspoon minced fresh turmeric or ¼ teaspoon ground*
- 1 *teaspoon roughly chopped lemongrass tops*
- 1 *teaspoon fish sauce*
- ½ *pound boneless pork loin or leg*

1. In a small skillet or saucepan, combine coconut milk, turmeric, lemongrass, and fish sauce. Bring to a boil, turn off heat, and allow to cool.

2. Slice pork ⅛ inch thick across the grain and cut into 1-inch squares. Marinate pork in coconut mixture 30 minutes. Thread meat on skewers, allowing 2 or 3 pork slices per skewer and stretching meat out in an even thin layer. Grill over a hot fire until lightly browned on both sides (about 2 minutes per side). Serve with Thai Fresh Chile Sauce (see page 35) or Peanut Sauce I or II (see page 36).

Serves 4 with other dishes.

For quick, even cooking, skewer thin strips of meat in a wave pattern, stretching the meat out along the skewer, as in this Thai pork saté.

Popular all over Southeast Asia, shrimp are especially tasty when grilled saté style. Baste during cooking with the chile-laced coconut-milk marinade.

SKEWERED MINCED LAMB
Magbub
Indonesia and Malaysia

Variations on this dish—seasoned minced lamb grilled on skewers—are found throughout the Moslem world, from Morocco to Indonesia. The tamarind in this version gives it a distinctively Southeast Asian flavor. A food processor makes short work of mincing the meat and blending the ingredients, or you can buy the meat already ground.

> 1 tablespoon oil
> ¼ cup minced onion or shallot
> 3 cloves garlic, minced
> 1 tablespoon minced ginger
> 1 teaspoon ground coriander
> Pinch ground cumin
> 1 pound boneless lamb shoulder, with some fat attached; or ground lamb
> 2 tablespoons coconut cream (see page 38)
> 1 tablespoon Tamarind Water (see page 34)
> ¼ teaspoon kosher salt
> Pinch palm sugar or brown sugar
> Oil, for grill

1. In a small skillet heat oil over low heat and cook onion, garlic, and ginger until onions become soft. Add coriander and cumin and remove from heat.

2. *To prepare in a food processor:* Cut lamb into cubes of about 1 inch, including some fat. Place in processor with onion mixture, coconut cream, Tamarind Water, salt, and sugar and chop with pulsing action until finely ground. *To prepare by hand:* Chop lamb by hand into pea-sized pieces (skip this step if using ground meat). Add onion mixture and mince all together to a fine texture. Transfer to a bowl, add coconut cream, Tamarind Water, salt, and sugar, and knead mixture by hand until smooth. Discard any large bits of gristle.

3. With moistened hands, roll lamb mixture into 1-inch balls. Skewer one or more meatballs on short skewers. Cover and refrigerate until ready to grill. The recipe may be prepared to this point up to 8 hours ahead.

4. Oil grill well and preheat thoroughly. Remove meat from refrigerator 15 minutes before cooking. Grill over a medium-hot fire until nicely browned all over, 7 to 10 minutes. Serve with Peanut Sauce I or II (see page 36).

Serves 4 with other dishes.

Variation Mold the meat around the skewers into sausage shapes about 3 inches long.

SHRIMP SATÉ
Saté udang
Indonesia

Shrimp paste gives this dish an extra punch. But be sure it is thoroughly incorporated into the marinade—if any lumps remain, they will taste unpleasantly strong in the finished dish. You might try it with the Cucumber Sauce on page 42.

> 4 cloves garlic, minced
> ¼ teaspoon shrimp paste
> ½ teaspoon minced fresh chile or ¼ teaspoon sambal ulek
> 1 tablespoon oil
> ⅓ cup medium coconut milk (see page 38)
> 1 tablespoon lemon or lime juice
> 1 teaspoon grated lemon or lime peel
> ½ teaspoon kosher salt
> 1 pound medium to large shrimp, peeled and deveined

1. Pound garlic, shrimp paste, and chile together first in a mortar.

2. In a small skillet heat oil over medium heat. Add garlic mixture and cook until strong smell dissipates. Remove from heat and stir in coconut milk, lemon juice, lemon peel, and salt. Allow to cool.

3. Thread shrimp passing skewer through each shrimp twice. Allow 2 to 4 shrimp per skewer, depending on size. Rub coconut mixture over shrimp and marinate 1 to 3 hours.

4. Grill shrimp over a medium-hot fire until meat is opaque white. Turn once during cooking and spread with any remaining marinade.

Serves 4 to 6 with other dishes.

INDONESIAN AND MALAYSIAN CUISINE

The legendary Spice Islands, the Indies that drew European merchants halfway around the world in search of pepper, cloves, cinnamon, and nutmeg, make up the modern nations of Indonesia and Malaysia. The two nations are closely related not only geographically but also ethnically and linguistically.

Indonesia, the former Dutch East Indies, is a predominantly Moslem country, except for the island of Bali, which clings to Hindu traditions. The population of Malaysia is more heterogeneous, consisting of Moslem Malays plus substantial Chinese and Indian minorities.

In both nations, blends of spices, onion, and ginger or one of its relatives (such as galangal or turmeric) flavor many dishes, and chile-flavored dishes and condiments known as sambals appear at most meals. Some authorities distinguish between the cooking of Java, site of the colonial capital, and the outer islands to the north and east.

In Java, where the colonial influence was strongest and the agricultural variety greatest, dishes tend to be more elaborate and a bit more mildly seasoned. Sumatran cooking—simpler but more spice-dominated—is typical of the outer islands. Malaysian cooking is more like that of Sumatra than that of Java, which is not surprising in view of their geographic proximity.

1. Thinly slice beef across the grain and cut slices into 1- by 3-inch pieces. Thread slices on skewers, stretching meat out in an even layer. In a small bowl, combine all remaining ingredients and rub mixture over beef. Marinate 30 minutes.

2. Grill over a hot fire until lightly browned, 1 to 2 minutes per side. Serve with Spicy Lime Sauce (see page 35) or a similar sauce.

Serves 4 with other dishes.

SPICED BEEF SATÉ
Saté bumbu
Indonesia

This form of *saté* is unique in two ways: The meat is cooked first in its sauce, then finished on the grill; and it is not served with a separate sauce.

> 1 tablespoon oil
> ½ cup diced onion
> 2 cloves garlic, minced
> 1 tablespoon minced ginger
> 1 fresh red chile, minced or ½ teaspoon sambal ulek
> 1 salam leaf or 2 curry leaves (optional)
> ½ teaspoon each ground turmeric and galangal
> 1 teaspoon ground coriander
> 2 macadamia nuts, ground (optional)
> 2 tablespoons Tamarind Water (see page 34)
> 1 tablespoon each kecap manis and water
> ¼ cup medium or thick coconut milk (see page 38)
> 1 pound tender beef (sirloin, rump, or top round), in 1-inch cubes
> Oil, for grill

1. In a skillet or wok, heat oil over medium-low heat. Add onion, garlic, ginger, chile, and salam leaf (if used) and cook slowly, stirring frequently, until onion softens. Add ground spices and macadamia nuts (if used) and cook until fragrant. Add liquids and beef and simmer until beef begins to spring back when pressed (rare to medium rare). Remove beef to a bowl and reduce sauce until quite thick. Remove from heat.

For saté bumbu, beef is first cooked in a currylike sauce, and only the final cooking takes place on the grill. It is an ideal dish to make ahead of time for an outdoor barbecue.

GRILLED BEEF, CAMBODIAN STYLE
Char kroeung
Cambodia

This milder version of *saté* uses Yellow Curry Paste, which contains no chile. If you prefer a hotter version, feel free to substitute a different curry paste (see pages 74-75); but bear in mind that this saté is meant to be served with a spicy sauce.

> ½ pound tender beef
> 2 tablespoons Yellow Curry Paste (see page 75)
> 1 teaspoon ground coriander seed
> 1 tablespoon fish sauce
> ½ teaspoon sugar
> 1 tablespoon oil
> ¼ cup medium or thick coconut milk (see page 38)

2. When meat is cool enough to handle, thread on skewers. Spread with reduced sauce. The recipe may be prepared to this point up to 4 hours ahead and kept covered in the refrigerator.

3. Oil grill well and preheat thoroughly. Grill meat over a medium-hot fire until nicely browned. Baste with sauce during cooking.

Serves 4 with other dishes.

Variation All sorts of variety meats can be cooked this way, although cooking times will vary. Cut beef or calves' liver into ½-inch cubes and cook in sauce only about 1 minute. Remove, reduce sauce, marinate, and grill as above, just until meat is medium rare. Or use lamb, veal, or beef heart cut into ½-inch cubes. Lamb and veal heart do not need to be cooked as directed in step 1.

GRILLED COCONUT CHICKEN
Ayam panggang
Indonesia

This dish is a cousin to Fried Coconut Chicken (see page 45). The chicken is mostly cooked by simmering in seasoned coconut milk, then given a final cooking by another method to brown the skin and add extra flavor.

- *1 whole broiling chicken (2 to 3 lb), see Note*
- *3 cloves garlic, minced*
- *½ cup minced onion*
- *2 tablespoons minced ginger*
- *1 fresh chile, minced or ½ teaspoon sambal ulek*
- *1 teaspoon kosher salt*
- *1 teaspoon ground coriander*
- *½ teaspoon ground turmeric*
- *1 tablespoon Tamarind Water (see page 34)*
- *2½ cups (14-oz can plus 6 oz water) medium coconut milk (see page 38)*
- *Coconut cream, skimmed from the medium coconut milk (optional)*
- *1 salam leaf or 2 curry leaves (optional)*

1. Split chicken down back and flatten; remove backbone or leave it attached, as desired. Remove kidneys, rinse chicken, and pat dry.

2. *To prepare in a mortar:* Pound garlic, onion, ginger, chile, and salt together to form a paste. *To prepare in a blender or food processor:* Add coconut cream as necessary to facilitate blending. Add coriander, turmeric, and Tamarind Water to paste. Rub paste all over chicken and set aside to marinate 30 minutes to 1 hour.

3. In a wok or deep skillet, heat all coconut milk and salam leaf (if used) over medium heat. Add chicken, along with its marinade, and simmer until meat becomes tender and juices show just a trace of pink. Remove chicken and reduce sauce until thick and oily.

4. Grill chicken skin-side down over a moderate charcoal fire until the skin is nicely browned, 5 to 8 minutes. Turn over and cook another 5 minutes. Cut into serving pieces, arrange on platter, and top with reduced sauce.

Serves 4 with other dishes.

Note Chicken legs, wings or other parts may be substituted, or use 2 Rock Cornish hens, split and grilled in the same way. If you wish to serve half a hen per person, divide the hens after grilling to prevent drying out of the breast meat.

Variation In step 4, the chicken may be broiled rather than grilled. Start with bone side toward heat, and finish with skin side. Allow a little less time or skin may burn.

SOY-GRILLED CHICKEN LEGS
Vietnam

With slight variations, this type of marinade for grilled chicken appears all over Southeast Asia. The cinnamon and the technique of partially boning the legs for faster grilling are Vietnamese touches. Instead of grilling, you can broil the chicken about 3 inches from the heat.

- *6 whole chicken legs*
- *2 cloves garlic*
- *1 tablespoon minced ginger*
- *2 teaspoons minced fresh lemongrass or 1 teaspoon lemongrass powder*
- *½ teaspoon ground coriander*
- *¼ teaspoon ground white pepper Pinch ground cinnamon*
- *3 tablespoons dark soy sauce*
- *½ teaspoon brown sugar*
- *1 tablespoon oil Nuoc Mam Sauce (see page 35), for accompaniment Assorted raw vegetables, for accompaniment*

1. Trim excess skin and fat from chicken legs. Place inner (skinless) side up on board. With a paring or boning knife, cut vertically along top of thigh bone to just beyond middle joint. Push thigh meat down to flatten slightly, exposing bone.

2. Pound garlic, ginger, and lemongrass together in a mortar, or mince together as finely as possible. In a bowl big enough to hold the chicken legs, combine coriander, pepper, cinnamon, soy sauce, sugar, and oil; stir to dissolve. Toss chicken legs in mixture and marinate 2 to 4 hours covered, in refrigerator, turning occasionally to marinate evenly.

3. Remove chicken from refrigerator at least 15 minutes before cooking. Grill over a medium-hot fire until meat springs back when pressed. Baste occasionally with marinade during cooking. Serve with Nuoc Mam Sauce and raw vegetables.

Serves 6 with other dishes.

Variation This marinade can be used for any cut of chicken or for birds split and flattened as in Grilled Coconut Chicken (see recipe at left).

CAMBODIAN AND LAOTIAN CUISINE

Two former kingdoms and former French colonies, Cambodia (Kampuchea) and Laos, are ethnically separate but share many culinary traits.

Modern Cambodia is just a remnant of the Khmer empire, which also covered most of Thailand and Laos from the ninth to the twelfth centuries. Many of the unifying features of the mainland cuisines stem from the Khmer period.

Cambodian cooking has a lightness and finesse that rivals the best of Thai and Vietnamese cooking. It shares certain traits with Laotian cuisine, including an emphasis on freshwater fish and shellfish rather than on seafood; a preference for glutinous (sticky) rice over other varieties; and a somewhat restrained use of chiles and spices, at least when compared to Thai cooking.

The Lao, the main ethnic group of Laos, are related culturally and linguistically to the Thai, and their cuisine shows close ties to that of northern Thailand. Much of the information on Laotian cooking in this book comes from a remarkable work, *Traditional Dishes of Laos* (Prospect Books, London, 1981). A translation of the manuscript notebooks of Phia Sing, late chef to the royal court and a sort of Laotian Renaissance man, this book gives a rare glimpse of a classic cuisine relatively unknown in the West.

RAW BEEF SALAD WITH ROASTED VEGETABLES
Lap
Laos and Thailand

Although the meat in this dish is served raw, it is combined with charcoal-roasted vegetables. In the traditional version, native to Laos and northern Thailand, *lap* is made of water-buffalo meat, and the vegetables are cooked in the ashes of a charcoal stove. Here beef and vegetables are cooked on a charcoal grill. This version is adapted from a recipe of Phia Sing in *Traditional Dishes of Laos* (see Cambodian and Laotian Cuisine, at left).

- 1 Japanese eggplant or 5 or 6 Thai eggplants, whole
- 3 shallots or 1 small yellow onion, whole
- 1 medium to large head garlic, whole
- 2 small dried chiles
- 1 stalk lemongrass
- 2 slices fresh galangal or 1 teaspoon ground
- ¼ pound beef or calves' liver
- ½ pound lean beef, preferably a flavorful cut such as round or sirloin tip
- 2 Kaffir lime leaves, soaked in warm water until soft, shredded as finely as possible (omit soaking step if using fresh leaves)
- 2 tablespoons Toasted Rice Powder (see page 65)
- 2 tablespoons fish sauce, or to taste
- 1 tablespoon finely chopped fresh coriander
- 1 red chile flower (optional, see Note)
  Butter or red-leaf lettuce leaves
  Lemon or lime wedges
- 1 tablespoon minced fresh chile

1. Prepare a hot charcoal fire. Grill whole eggplant, shallots, and garlic until skins are burnt; remove and set aside to cool. Grill dried chiles until they begin to darken; set aside. Grill lemongrass and fresh galangal (if used) until quite fragrant; set aside.

2. Slice liver thinly and grill slices just until done. Set aside to cool, then cut into julienne strips.

3. When vegetables are cool enough to handle, peel away burnt parts. Separate garlic into cloves and peel. Discard seeds from chiles, if desired. Remove tough outer leaves and tops of lemongrass and slice remainder as finely as possible. Add galangal (mince if using fresh) and grind all together to a paste in a mortar, food processor, or blender.

4. Chop beef as finely as possible by hand or in food processor; discard gristle. In a bowl, combine meat with pounded paste, liver, lime leaves, rice powder, and fish sauce and blend thoroughly. Taste; adjust seasoning. Mound mixture on a plate and garnish with coriander and a chile flower, if desired. To serve salad, wrap spoonfuls in lettuce leaves and season to taste with lemon juice and minced fresh chile.

Serves 8 with other dishes.

<u>Note</u> To make a chile flower, cut three or four lengthwise slits in a slender red chile from near the stem to the tip; soak it in cold water until the "petals" curl.

BONELESS STUFFED CHICKEN
Rellenong manok
Philippines

Although roasting is not a traditional Southeast Asian technique, Filipino cooks have been quick to adapt Western roasted dishes. Experienced cooks will recognize this dish as a variation of the French *galantine*.

- 1 large whole frying chicken (about 4 lb)
- 2 tablespoons soy sauce
  Juice of 1 lemon
- ½ pound boneless ham, in one piece
- 1 pound boneless pork, not too lean (shoulder with most of visible fat removed is ideal)
- ½ cup chopped onion
- 2 tablespoons minced garlic
- 2 uncooked eggs
- 3 tablespoons raisins
- ¼ cup each finely diced carrots and sweet or dill pickles
- ½ teaspoon freshly ground pepper
- 3 hard-cooked eggs, peeled

1. Place chicken on a large cutting board. Cut off wings at elbow joint, and remove feet and neck if present. Remove large pieces of fat from cavity and neck area.

2. Place chicken breast side down on board. With a sharp boning or paring knife, cut through skin along backbone. Peel skin back a little on one side, cutting away meat from bones. When hip and shoulder joints are exposed, twist or cut them away from carcass, being careful not to tear skin. Leave leg and wing alone for now and concentrate on cutting the breast free from breastbone. Be especially careful not to puncture skin lying across breastbone. Repeat on other side, then lift carcass away from skin, carefully cutting skin free from ridge of breastbone.

3. Cut and scrape thigh meat away to expose thigh bone; remove bone. Leave wing and drumstick bones in place. You should now be left with a whole skin and most of the meat. Remove thigh meat and any loose pieces of breast meat and set aside for stuffing, along with any large bits on carcass. Leave main parts of breast attached to skin.

4. Combine soy sauce and lemon juice and rub all over chicken skin. Set aside to marinate while preparing stuffing.

5. Preheat oven to 350° F. Cut half the ham into sticks about ¼ inch thick and set aside. Combine remaining ham with pork, chicken leg meat, onion, and garlic and grind together in a food processor or through the finest disk of a meat grinder. Transfer to a bowl and combine with uncooked eggs, raisins, carrots, pickles, and pepper. Sauté a small patty of the mixture in a skillet and taste for seasoning; adjust if necessary.

6. Lay out boned chicken on a large plate, skin-side down. Spread half the filling over skin, molding it into thigh cavities. Place hard-cooked eggs end to end down the middle and

lay ham strips alongside. Add remaining filling, molding it into a loaf shape around eggs. Bring skin together over filling and sew up opening, completely encasing filling.

7. Place chicken breast side up on a rack in a roasting pan. Roast, basting occasionally with its own juices, until skin is golden brown and filling has reached an internal temperature of 165° F (insert thermometer into stuffing off-center to avoid eggs). Allow to rest at least 30 minutes, covered loosely with foil, before carving. To carve, remove legs and stitches and cut across into thick slices. Serve hot or lukewarm, or refrigerate overnight and serve cold.

Serves 6 to 8 with other dishes.

Boneless Stuffed Chicken, rellenong manok, is a European-style galantine transported to the Philippines by the Spanish and modified by generations of native cooks.

AN INDONESIAN
OUTDOOR BUFFET

*Fish Grilled in
Banana Leaves*

*Chicken Saté With
Sweet Soy Sauce*

Chile-Fried Squid

*Vegetable Curry With Coconut Milk
(see page 80)*

*Mixed Vegetable Salad With
Peanut Sauce (see page 116)*

*Sticky Rice Rolls
(see page 104)*

Beer and soft drinks

---

*Although the Indonesian
rijsttafel is now out of
fashion (see page 8), the
tradition of gracious
entertaining is timeless.
Buffet service is ideal for this
kind of food, as it allows
each diner to sample a bit of
this and a bit of that. Here is
a casual buffet for a warm
summer evening, centered
around the charcoal grill.
Only the squid sambal is
extremely hot; but it serves
as a condiment more than
as a dish.*

FISH GRILLED IN BANANA LEAVES

Rich, oily fish are best for this treatment. If possible, use small fish that can be cooked whole because the bones give extra succulence to the meat. Small mackerel, butterfish, and larger varieties of sardine and herring are ideal. The recipe also works with fillets or chunks of larger mackerel or bonito.

  1½ to 2 pounds whole fish (see list above)
  ¼ cup diced green or yellow onion
  3 cloves garlic, minced
  1 tablespoon minced ginger
  ½ teaspoon kosher salt
    Banana leaves
  2 to 3 fresh red or green chiles, sliced
  1 lemon or lime, peeled and thinly sliced
    Fresh coriander sprigs (optional)

1. Have fish cleaned and scaled if necessary. Leave heads on if they will fit inside packages. Rinse fish well and pat dry.

2. In a mortar, pound onion, garlic, ginger, and salt together to a paste. Or mince together as finely as possible, then mash to a paste with the side of a knife blade. Spread mixture over fish.

3. Place fish in the middle of a large square of banana leaf or aluminum foil. (Small fish may be wrapped two or more to a package, overlapping slightly if necessary.) Top with sliced chiles, lemon slices, and coriander (if used), and fold into rectangular packages as directed on page 66. Grill over a medium-hot fire, allowing 10 minutes per inch of thickness of the fish.

Serves 4 with other dishes.

Fish Baked in Banana Leaves

Preheat oven to 450° F. Prepare fish packages as directed above. Measure fish at its thickest part and bake packages on a sheet pan, allowing 10 to 12 minutes per inch of thickness.

CHICKEN SATÉ WITH SWEET SOY SAUCE
Saté ayam manis

Sweet soy-based marinades are among the most popular for chicken, beef, or lamb *saté*. Try the chicken by itself before adding a peanut sauce—you might prefer it just as it is.

  2 cloves garlic, minced
    Juice of ½ lime
  2 tablespoons kecap manis
  1 whole chicken breast, skinned, boned, cut into ¾-inch cubes

In a small bowl, combine garlic, lime juice, and kecap manis. Marinate chicken cubes in this mixture 1 hour. Thread on skewers, 4 or 5 cubes each, and grill until meat is firm, 3 to 5 minutes.

Serves 4 with other dishes.

Variation Just about any tender cut of meat can be prepared this way. Cut beef steaks, pork loin, or leg of lamb across the grain into ¼-inch-thick slices about 1 by 3 inches. Thread meat lengthwise on skewers, stretching it out to an even thickness. Chicken livers can be grilled whole; cut beef or pork liver into strips about ⅜ inch thick.

CHILE-FRIED SQUID
Sambal cumi-cumi

In its most authentic form, this sambal is bright red with chile and quite hot. If you prefer it a little milder, use fresh chiles that are not too hot, such as the milder strain of jalapeños now on the market; otherwise, use less chile and make up the color difference with paprika.

  ½ pound squid
  ½ cup diced onion
  2 cloves garlic, minced
  3 or 4 semihot fresh red chiles, minced, or 1 teaspoon sambal ulek
  ½ teaspoon kosher salt
  2 tablespoons oil
  1 teaspoon paprika, if needed
  2 tablespoons Tamarind Water (see page 34) or lemon juice

1. Clean squid as directed on page 55. Remove purplish outer skin and cut sacs into rings.

2. *To prepare in a mortar:* Pound onion, garlic, chiles, and salt together to a coarse paste. *To prepare in a blender or food processor:* Grind together with oil.

3. In a wok or skillet, heat oil over low heat and add paste. (If oil was used in grinding paste, add paste to dry pan.) Cook slowly until quite fragrant and oil is well stained with red. Add paprika if necessary to enhance color.

4. Turn heat to medium-high, add squid and Tamarind Water, and cook just until squid is done (about 2 minutes). Serve hot or at room temperature.

Serves 4 to 6 with other dishes.

This transportable Indonesian meal is suitable for backyard or beach: rice rolls, squid sambal, a curry, and a salad are prepared ahead and later served at room temperature; the chicken saté and leaf-wrapped fish are brought in a cooler and grilled on the spot.

Rice is the most indispensable food in Southeast Asia. It may be cooked as a grain or ground and made into noodles or paperlike sheets.

Rice, Noodles & Salads

Rice is *the* staple of Southeast Asian cuisines, appearing in a variety of guises. In this chapter you'll find a broad selection of recipes for this basic food and for equally versatile noodles, from perfect plain rice (see page 101) to elaborate leaf-wrapped dishes (see page 104), from simple egg noodles (see page 107) to meal-in-a-dish presentations (see page 110). Salads provide variety in meals. Among the offerings here are unusual salads of green tea leaves (see page 115) and ginger (see page 113). A special section (see page 118) features foods in edible wrappers, such as lumpia. Finally, for an exotic afternoon snack, try the sweet and savory tidbits in the Philippine Merienda menu on page 122.

Most Southeast Asian meals include rice in some form. Usually it is served plain, preferably unsalted, as a filling staple, a background for highly seasoned dishes, or a vehicle for sauces. As befits such an important staff of life, rice is often served in a fancy container, such as this highly decorated dish from Thailand. A cover (not shown) keeps the rice warm between servings.

RICE

The hundreds of varieties of rice grown in Asia can be loosely grouped into three categories: long grain, short grain, and glutinous. Besides obvious differences in shape, the varieties differ in the composition of starches in the grain. This determines how the grains swell in cooking and how much they stick together.

Because most people in Southeast Asia eat rice with a spoon or fork rather than with chopsticks, stickiness of the grains is less important than it is in China or Japan. Still, the Asian taste is for softer, clingier grains than Westerners are used to.

Long-grain Also known as *patna* rice, long-grain rice is the type most familiar to Americans and the one most favored in Southeast Asia. It is the least sticky type, cooking into fluffy, almost separate grains. Where rice is eaten with a spoon or fork, long-grain is ideal; it can also be eaten with chopsticks if properly cooked. Most of the rice grown in the southern United States is of this type, and large sacks of Texas long-grain

rice are a common sight in Asian markets. Some Asian varieties are known for their special fragrance; the jasmine rice of Thailand is a good example, although its aroma seems more nutty than flowery. Parboiled (converted) rice is not suitable for Asian-style recipes, as it produces a bowl of totally un-Asian grains that will not stick together no matter how they are cooked.

Short- and medium-grain These types include several with smaller grains that are more oval than long-grain rice. Most cook up softer and stickier than long grain, with a slightly fuller and sweeter flavor. This type is less popular in Southeast Asia, except in areas where rice is normally eaten with chopsticks or used in compressed-rice dishes such as Indonesian Rice Packets (see page 104). However, if you prefer a more flavorful rice, you might experiment with the short- and medium-grain types widely grown in California. The Calrose variety is typical, offering a compromise between firm and soft, separate and sticky. All the shorter varieties require less water for cooking than does the long-grain rice.

Glutinous This is a special category of short-grain rice, also known as sweet or sticky rice. It is not interchangeable with other short-grain varieties. True to its name it cooks to the softest and stickiest consistency of all, though the taste is not noticeably sweeter than that of other rice. In some areas of Southeast Asia, particularly where most foods are eaten with fingers, glutinous rice is the everyday favorite. In most of the region, however, it is used for special purposes. It may be sweetened to make various cakes and confections, or molded into balls, logs, or other shapes, with sweet or savory fillings. It is especially valued because it can stand at room temperature for several hours without getting hard, an advantage when rice is cooked once a day for several meals. Glutinous rice is typically steamed, either in addition to or instead of boiling (see Glutinous Rice I and II, opposite page).

Brown Although nutritionally superior to white rice, brown rice is not popular among Asians. White rice is considered easier to digest, especially in the quantities typical of the Southeast Asian diet. However, you can serve long, medium, or short brown rice with your Asian meals.

COOKING RICE

Asian-style rice is either boiled or steamed. What is usually called steamed rice is, in fact, cooked by the absorption method, described at right. True steamed rice takes longer to cook, and the absorption method is nearly foolproof.

An electric rice cooker is a common feature in many modern Asian kitchens. These appliances cook rice to a perfect consistency every time, and they free a stove burner for other uses. If you cook a lot of Asian-style meals, an electric rice cooker is a handy item to have.

Asian-style rice is never salted. Many of the dishes served with rice have plenty of salt. Although some Westerners may find unsalted rice too bland, in Southeast Asian cuisines the very blandness of rice is a virtue: It does not add to or subtract from the accompanying dishes, but merely serves as a background. If you prefer to add salt to your rice, decrease the salt in other dishes accordingly.

Asian cooks always wash rice thoroughly before cooking to remove excess starch. Most rice comes from the mill with a light dusting of starch to absorb moisture and keep the grains fresh, but most rice packages now say that washing is not necessary. Washing removes some nutrients from rice, but finicky cooks insist on washing anyway, saying it gives the rice a "cleaner" taste. Try it both ways and decide for yourself.

When planning meals, allow anywhere from ⅓ cup to ¾ cup of uncooked rice per person, depending on taste and appetite. Glutinous rice is considered more filling, so it is traditionally served in smaller quantities. Leftover rice may be reheated by steaming, made into a breakfast porridge or used for fried rice (see recipes on page 102).

GLUTINOUS RICE I

In Thailand and Laos, glutinous rice is cooked entirely by steaming. This results in more separate grains than would boiling, but the rice is still sticky enough to be molded together.

Glutinous rice (about ⅓ cup uncooked rice per serving)
1½ cups water for first cup rice, 1 cup for each additional cup rice

1. Wash rice in several changes of water until water runs clear. Drain. Place rice in a bowl, cover with water, and soak 1 to 12 hours. Drain.

2. Line a steamer basket or colander with moistened cheesecloth (this in unnecessary if your steamer has very small holes). Spread rice in basket in an even layer. Steam over rapidly boiling water for 25 minutes. Serve hot, warm, or at room temperature. To keep warm, turn off heat under steamer, let steam dissipate, replace cover, and let stand until ready.

GLUTINOUS RICE II

In this version the rice is boiled first, then finished in a steamer. The result is stickier than the simply steamed version.

Glutinous rice (about ⅓ cup uncooked rice per serving)
1½ cups water for first cup rice, 1 cup for each additional cup rice

1. Wash rice in several changes of water until water runs clear. Drain. Place rice in a pot with water. Cover, bring to boil, reduce heat, and simmer 15 minutes. Turn off heat and let stand covered another 15 minutes.

2. Prepare steamer as in step 2 of previous recipe. Steam rice 15 minutes. Serve hot, warm, or at room temperature.

"STEAMED" RICE

Instructions for cooking rice by the absorption method, commonly but incorrectly known as "steamed rice," are approximate. The rice may require more or less water depending on the depth of the pot, the strain of rice, and even the age of the rice (older rice takes more water). The amount also makes a difference; twice as much rice does not mean twice as much water. As a rule of thumb, use the following measurements: For long-grain rice, 2 cups water for the first cup of rice, 1 cup water for each additional cup. For medium- or short-grain rice, 1½ cups water for the first cup, 1 cup water for each additional cup.

1. Measure rice into bowl. Cover with cold water. Swirl with your hand several times until water becomes cloudy. Pour out water, using a hand-held strainer to catch grains. Repeat washing procedure until water is clear, 3 to 5 times in all. Drain rice thoroughly and transfer to cooking pot. Cover with cold water 1 inch deeper than depth of rice. Use more water with long-grain rice.

2. Bring to a boil, cover, reduce heat, and simmer until water is absorbed, about 15 minutes for short- or medium-grain rice, 18 for long-grain. Lift cover only long enough to check that rice has absorbed water, then cover again. Turn off heat, let stand 10 minutes, and fluff.

BASIC FRIED RICE
Nasi goreng
Indonesia

Popular throughout Asia, fried rice offers an endless variety of ways to use leftover rice. Here is a simple version to serve as a side dish.

- *1 small onion or 2 shallots, minced*
- *1 teaspoon minced garlic*
- *1 teaspoon dried shrimp paste*
- *½ teaspoon sambal ulek or minced fresh chile*
- *2 tablespoons oil*
- *3 cups cooked rice*
- *2 tablespoons dark soy sauce or kecap manis*
- *Salt, to taste*
- *Sliced green onions, for garnish*

1. In a mortar, pound onion, garlic, shrimp paste, and sambal ulek together to a paste.

2. Heat oil in a wok over medium heat. Add paste and cook, stirring, until fragrant. Add rice to pan and stir to break up clumps. Turn heat to medium high and stir-fry vigorously, scraping up any bits of rice that cling to pan. When rice begins to brown, add soy sauce and salt to taste. Continue stir-frying until liquid is nearly all evaporated. Serve garnished with green onions.

Serves 4 with other dishes.

COCONUT RICE

Rice is often cooked in coconut milk for added flavor and richness. Long-grain, short-grain, or glutinous rice may be cooked this way, with the type of rice determining the amount of liquid. Use thick or thin coconut milk according to taste. If the rice is too rich when made with straight canned coconut milk, thin it with half its volume of water. One 14-ounce can plus 6 to 7 ounces water is sufficient for 1½ cups long-grain rice.

- *1½ cups rice*
- *2¼ cups thin coconut milk (see page 38)*
- *1 salam leaf (optional)*
- *Fried Onion Flakes (see page 35), for garnish*

Follow the directions for "Steamed" Rice (see page 101), substituting coconut milk for water. Add the salam leaf (if used) just before covering the pot, and remove it before serving. Some coconut cream will rise to the surface; stir it in before serving. Top with Fried Onion Flakes.

Yellow Rice Yellow-tinged rice, a traditional part of wedding feasts and other celebrations in Indonesia and Malaysia, can be served up anytime you want to add a colorful touch to any meal. Just add ¼ teaspoon ground turmeric to the liquid in the above recipe.

RICE PORRIDGE WITH SALTED EGGS

Of Chinese origin, rice porridge is served for breakfast all over Southeast Asia. It is known as *congee* to the English-speaking residents of Asia and as *jook* in Cantonese. By itself it is unbelievably bland, so it is always served with salty additions such as pickled vegetables, Chinese sausage, salt-preserved eggs, or leftover meats liberally seasoned with soy sauce.

- *¼ cup uncooked rice*
- *3 cups water*
- *2 salt-preserved eggs (see Note, page 47), hard-cooked*
- *¼ cup sliced green onions*

Wash rice and place in a heavy covered pan. Add water, bring to a boil, cover, and reduce heat to the lowest possible setting. Simmer, stirring occasionally, until rice is very soft and liquid thickens (about 2 hours). Peel eggs and cut into slices or wedges. Serve in deep bowls topped with eggs and green onions.

Serves 2.

<u>Note</u> Congee can also be made with leftover cooked rice; just add more water and simmer until very tender. Whether you are using raw or cooked rice, the amount of water may be varied to produce a thinner or thicker porridge.

SPECIAL FRIED RICE
Nasi goreng istimewa
Indonesia

A fancier version of fried rice, this can be a one-dish meal or part of a larger menu. Other meats and vegetables can be substituted or added.

- *¼ pound tender beef*
- *1 tablespoon kecap manis*
- *4 tablespoons oil*
- *2 eggs, lightly beaten*
- *1 tablespoon minced garlic*
- *2 fresh red chiles or 1 red bell pepper, seeds and veins removed, diced*
- *3 tablespoons dried shrimp, soaked in water 15 minutes, drained, and minced*
- *¼ pound shrimp, peeled and deveined*
- *3 cups cooked rice*
- *½ cup each sliced cabbage and diced tomato*
- *1 tablespoon fish sauce*
- *Sliced green onions, for garnish*
- *Red chile flower, for garnish (optional, see Note, page 94)*

1. Thinly slice beef across grain and cut into narrow 1½-inch strips. In a small bowl combine with kecap manis and marinate 15 minutes.

2. Heat a wok or large skillet over medium heat and add 2 tablespoons of the oil. Add eggs and swirl pan to form a thin omelet. When eggs are almost set, remove the omelet to a plate and set aside. When cool cut into thin strips.

3. Add remaining 2 tablespoons oil to pan. Add garlic, chiles, and dried shrimp and stir-fry until fragrant. Add shrimp and beef and stir-fry until shrimp begins to turn pink. Add rice to pan and stir to break up clumps. Turn heat to medium-high and stir-fry vigorously, scraping up any bits of rice that cling to pan. When rice begins to brown, stir in cabbage and tomato and continue stir-frying until mixture is nearly dry. Sprinkle with fish sauce and transfer to serving platter, heaping rice into a tall cone. Garnish with green onions and egg strips and top with red chile flower.

Serves 4 to 6 with other dishes.

Indonesian-style Special Fried Rice is a satisfying one-dish lunch or supper. For an elaborate buffet, it is traditionally served in a cone shape.

Lemper is a popular snack food, a sort of sandwich in which sticky rice serves as the bread. Stuffings may be sweet or savory; this version uses a cooked spiced-chicken mixture.

STICKY RICE ROLLS
Lemper
Indonesia and Malaysia

In Southeast Asia these rice rolls are popular as a snack. They are also ideal for picnics, as they can be made ahead of time and served at room temperature. The spiced chicken filling is typical of Indonesia, but the possibilities are endless: cooked or raw vegetables, leftover curries, even fruits. The proportions of rice to filling can also be varied.

> 2 *cups glutinous rice*
> 2 *cups water*
> 1 *cup thick coconut milk (see page 38)*
> 2 *tablespoons coconut cream, skimmed from the thick coconut milk*
> 2 *shallots*
> 2 *cloves garlic*
> 1 *teaspoon ground coriander*
> *Pinch each salt and sugar*
> 1 *tablespoon oil*
> 1 *Kaffir lime leaf*
> 1 *salam leaf*
> 1 *whole chicken breast, boned, skinned, and finely diced*
> *Pinch turmeric*
> *Banana leaves*

1. Cook rice in water and skimmed coconut milk as described in "Steamed" Rice, on page 101. While rice is cooking prepare filling (steps 2 and 3).

2. Mince shallots and garlic together as finely as possible by hand or pound to a paste in a mortar. If using a mortar, add coriander, salt, and sugar with paste; otherwise combine in a small bowl.

3. In a skillet or wok, heat oil over medium-low heat. Add lime leaf, salam leaf, and shallot-garlic mixture and cook until fragrant. Add chicken, coconut cream, and turmeric and cook until chicken is done and mixture is nearly dry. Taste for seasoning and adjust if necessary. Discard lime and salam leaves.

4. Lay out four 8- by 12-inch pieces of banana leaf or aluminum foil. In center of each spread a quarter of the cooked rice into a 4- by 8-inch rectangle about ½ inch thick. Arrange a quarter of the chicken mixture down the middle of the rectangle, lengthwise, and roll the foil or leaf into a tight 12-inch cylinder. Seal ends (use a toothpick or string to secure ends if using leaves). Chill 4 hours to overnight before serving. Serve at room temperature, or heat 15 minutes in a steamer or on a grill. To serve, unwrap roll and cut into thick slices. For easier slicing moisten knife blade before each cut and slice with a gentle sawing motion.

Serves 4 with other dishes.

RICE PACKETS
Lontong
Indonesia

When rice is cooked in a closed container, the grains swell together to form a firm mass that keeps its shape after unmolding. Whether the container is a banana leaf, a basket woven of fresh palm fronds, or even a sheet of aluminum foil, the effect is the same: a block of firm rice that can be sliced and eaten with fingers. Lontong are especially useful for picnics or other informal meals when you want to keep cutlery to a minimum. Traditionally the packets are filled with uncooked rice and boiled for several hours. In this adaptation, the rice is partially cooked first, then wrapped and steamed.

> 2 cups uncooked rice (a
>   medium-grain rice such as
>   the Calrose variety is ideal)
> 5 cups water
> 4 pieces banana leaf

1. Wash rice and combine with water in a covered pan. Cover, bring to a boil, reduce heat, and simmer 15 minutes. Turn off heat and let stand 15 to 30 minutes longer. Rice will still be quite moist.

2. *To prepare with banana leaves:* Pour boiling water over leaves to soften them; drain. Lay out a square of leaf with the grain running sideways. Spoon a quarter of the cooked rice onto the leaf an inch or two from the near edge, leaving at least 2 inches at each end. Roll up leaf, forming an open-ended cylinder. Pinch one end of roll shut and fold flattened portion of leaf over top. Secure with a string or narrow strip of banana leaf. Seal and tie the other end in the same way. *To prepare with aluminum foil:* Roll rice in 12-inch pieces of aluminum foil, rolling up ends of foil to seal. Tying is unnecessary.

3. Bring water in a steamer to a rolling boil. Steam rolls 1 hour; check water level periodically and add more boiling water if neccesary. Remove rolls from steamer and chill at least 6 hours. Serve cold or at room temperature, unwrapped and sliced into ½-inch slices.

Serves 4 to 6 with other dishes.

Variation Use Coconut Rice (see page 102) prepared with ½ cup extra water per cup of rice in place of the plain rice in the above recipe.

"POT-ROASTED" RICE
Com chien
Vietnam

"Pot-roasted" is the usual translation of the Vietnamese name of this dish, but the technique is basically that of the Middle Eastern pilaf. The use of butter in this recipe is a sign of the French influence in Indochina.

> 2 cups long-grain rice
> 2 tablespoons butter or oil
> 2½ cups water

Wash rice if desired and drain thoroughly. In a heavy covered pan, melt butter over medium heat. When foam begins to subside, stir in rice and cook, stirring, until rice becomes opaque and takes on a slight golden tinge. Add water, cover, bring to a boil, reduce heat to low, and simmer 15 minutes. Turn off heat and let stand covered another 10 minutes. Fluff with a fork or chopsticks before serving.

Serves 4 to 6.

For a particularly portable form of rice, wrap partially cooked grains in banana-leaf packages and steam them. The result is lontong, nearly solid rolls of rice suitable for slicing and eating with fingers.

This assortment of Southeast Asian noodles includes rice noodles, the wide and narrow noodles at upper right, and the precooked pancit luglug at lower left. Small and large bundles of bean threads are at bottom. The sticklike noodles at upper left are eggless and made from wheat flour. To their right are precooked egg noodles, pancit canton. The others are dried egg noodles in various sizes and shapes.

NOODLES

Southeast Asians are among the most pasta-loving people on earth. Noodles made of wheat flour, rice flour, or bean starch are second only to rice as a basic food throughout the region. They may be served hot or cold; they may be boiled, stir-fried, deep-fried, or simmered in soup; or they may be added to curries, stews, salads, and even stuffings. Noodlelike doughs are used to wrap all sorts of foods, to be eaten plain or formed into packages to be fried.

If you live near an Asian neighborhood, you should be able to get all sorts of fresh Asian-style noodles and wrappers, and most well-stocked supermarkets carry some varieties. Dried varieties are also available by mail order (see page 33). Or you can make your own from the recipes on the following pages.

Noodle shapes and names vary, but in terms of cooking technique they can be grouped together according to the type of starch they are made of: wheat flour, rice flour, or bean starch. In general, wheat and rice noodles are boiled, if only briefly, before other treatments, and bean-starch noodles are simply soaked in warm water.

Wheat-flour noodles may be made entirely of flour and water, or they may contain some egg; however, they are generally made with less egg than Western-style egg noodles. In Southeast Asia, they are used mainly in Chinese-style dishes such as Stir-Fried Two Noodles (see page 110). In the following recipes, "thin egg noodles" means a noodle less than $\frac{1}{16}$ inch thick, the type sold in Asian markets in sealed plastic packages as Chinese-style noodles or extrathin *mein*. Homemade noodles cut on the narrowest cutter are a good substitute; dried vermicelli or thin Japanese *ramen* may also be used. If you prefer a thicker noodle, look for the regular Chinese noodles, which are about as thick as spaghetti.

Pancit Canton is a dish (see page 109) as well as a special type of noodle used in the Philippines. This thick egg noodle has been precooked and dried, so it only needs reheating in a sauce.

Rice-flour noodles also come in several forms. Both narrow and wide noodles are sold dried, labeled rice vermicelli or rice sticks. In the recipes in this book, "rice sticks" refers to the narrow variety, about 1/16 inch wide, and "flat rice noodles" means the wider type, about 1/8 inch wide. In Asian stores, the wider type is often found in packages labeled with the Thai name *chantaboon*. Fresh rice noodles are sold in well-stocked Asian markets in plastic-wrapped trays; or you can make your own (see Fresh Rice Noodles, page 109).

Bean threads—sometimes known as either cellophane noodles, glass noodles, pea-starch noodles, or Chinese vermicelli—are thin, semi-transparent noodles made from mung bean starch (the bean used to make bean sprouts). They do not need to be cooked, merely soaked until soft. Unlike other noodles, however, they can simmer along with braised meats for an hour or more without falling apart, all the time absorbing flavor. Do not soak bean threads any longer than necessary to soften them or they will absorb too much water. Bean threads can also be fried without any preliminary soaking. Just a few seconds in hot oil turns them into crisp white sticks, good for garnishing other dishes or as a base for a salad.

BOILING NOODLES

Many recipes call for noodles that have been boiled prior to stir-frying or braising. If you are using home-made or packaged fresh egg noodles, fluff them a little first to loosen the clumps, then drop them into a large pot of lightly salted water at a rolling boil. Stir immediately with long chopsticks or a spoon to separate the noodles, and begin testing them as soon as the water returns to the boil; most will be done within a few seconds. Dried noodles take longer, although precise cooking time varies with the size and from one brand to another. Rice noodles generally need no preliminary boiling if they are to be cooked in a sauce, as in Pad Thai (see page 112).

Drain cooked noodles in a colander in the sink and, unless you plan to sauce them immediately, rinse with cold water to prevent further cooking. Toss the noodles under running water by hand so you can feel when they are thoroughly cooled. Drain well and toss with a little oil to keep them from sticking. If sufficiently oiled and tightly wrapped, noodles can be kept several hours or even overnight, covered, in the refrigerator.

FRESH EGG NOODLES

Making your own dough for Chinese noodles is a snap with an Italian-style pasta maker. It can also be made by hand with a rolling pin, although this technique requires a little practice.

1 large egg
2 tablespoons water
1 cup all-purpose flour (approximately)
¼ cup cornstarch

1. Combine egg and water in a medium-sized bowl and beat lightly with a fork or chopstick. Stir in ¾ cup of the flour and mix until dough forms clumps.

2. Turn out dough onto a board dusted with remaining flour. Knead until smooth, kneading in remaining flour. Add more flour only if necessary to keep dough from sticking. Invert bowl over dough and let rest 15 to 30 minutes.

3. *To prepare dough with a pasta machine:* Scrape board clean and dust with cornstarch. Divide dough into 2 or 4 pieces for easier handling, if desired. Set rollers at widest setting.

Flatten a piece of dough by hand to about ¼ inch thick, dust with cornstarch, and roll out to a thin oval. Fold each end over the middle, forming three layers. Dust outside again and roll. Repeat 4 or 5 times until dough is smooth, stretchy, and pliable. Turn rollers to next smaller setting and roll out once (do not fold). Continue rolling, reducing thickness one setting with each roll, until dough is the desired thickness. If rolls become too long to handle easily, cut in half and continue rolling with each piece. *To prepare dough by hand:* Scrape board clean and dust with cornstarch. Divide dough in half and set one piece aside. Flatten the other piece by hand to about ¼ inch thick, then roll out into a large oval with a rolling pin. Dust dough with cornstarch as necessary to prevent sticking. Starting at one edge, wrap a little dough around the pin and roll toward center, trapping a layer of dough between the pin and the rest of the dough. Roll pin back and forth several times with both palms against the pin, stretching the dough sideways along the pin. Roll another few inches of dough around the pin and repeat the process. When you reach the middle of the sheet, unroll the dough, turn it around, and repeat from the other end. Roll finished sheet to reduce any thick spots.

4. Spread rolled sheets out to dry on a table, on clean towels, or drape them over the back of a chair. Allow to dry slightly, but not so much that they become brittle. Cut sheets into noodles of desired size with cutter attachment of pasta machine, or by rolling a sheet up from one end and cutting the roll into narrow coils. Noodles may be cooked right away or dusted with additional cornstarch and allowed to dry for several hours.

Makes about ½ pound noodles.

Pancit Canton, as the name implies, shows a strong Chinese influence. In fact this Philippine noodle dish is a version of Cantonese chow mein.

PANCIT CANTON
Philippines

This dish resembles Cantonese chow mein, but in the Philippine manner liquid is added to the pan before the noodles. Because they are precooked, *pancit canton* noodles (which share their name with this dish) need no preliminary soaking or cooking before being added to the sauce.

- 1 egg white
- 1 teaspoon soy sauce
- 1 teaspoon cornstarch
- 1 chicken breast, diced
- 1 tablespoon oil
- 2 Chinese sausages, sliced ¼ inch thick
- ¼ pound shrimp, peeled and deveined if necessary
- ½ cup diced onion
- 2 tablespoons minced garlic
- 1 tablespoon minced ginger
- 1½ cups Basic Chicken Stock (see page 62)
- 1 tablespoon fish sauce
- ¼ teaspoon freshly ground pepper
- 6 to 8 ounces dried precooked egg noodles (pancit canton) or thick egg noodles, boiled, drained, and oiled
- ½ cup snow peas
- ¼ cup each sliced bamboo shoots and shredded carrots
- ½ teaspoon Chinese or Japanese sesame oil

1. In a small bowl, combine egg white, soy sauce, and cornstarch and blend thoroughly. Toss chicken cubes in mixture and marinate 30 minutes.

2. Heat wok over medium heat and add oil. Add sliced sausages and stir-fry until browned; remove from pan. Stir-fry shrimp just until they change color and remove. Drain chicken cubes of excess marinade and stir-fry until firm; remove.

3. Add onion, garlic, and ginger to wok and cook until fragrant. Add stock, fish sauce, and pepper, bring to a boil, and reduce by half. Add noodles, vegetables, and meats and cook until noodles have absorbed most of liquid. Turn off heat, sprinkle with sesame oil, and serve.

Serves 4 with other dishes.

BRAISED RICE NOODLES WITH PORK AND SHRIMP
Pancit bihon guisado
Philippines

In this dish, rice sticks (*bihon*) are soaked until soft, then cooked in a sauce until they absorb most of the liquid. Use thin egg noodles and the dish becomes *pancit mami guisado.*

- ½ pound raw shrimp, preferably with heads on
- 1½ cups Basic Chicken Stock (see page 62)
- 1 tablespoon annatto seeds, cracked in mortar (optional)
- 2 tablespoons oil
- 2 tablespoons minced garlic
- 1 small onion, minced
- ½ pound cooked and shredded pork
  Soy or fish sauce, to taste
  Freshly ground pepper, to taste
- ½ pound rice sticks, soaked in warm water until soft and drained
- 1½ cups vegetables (a variety of the following): sliced cabbage or celery, shredded carrots, trimmed snow peas, blanched and sliced green beans
- 1 hard-cooked egg, sliced, for garnish
  Fresh coriander, for garnish

1. Peel shrimp, reserving heads and shells, and devein if necessary. Place shells and heads in a saucepan with stock and annatto seeds, if used. Bring to a boil, reduce heat; simmer 10 minutes; strain and reserve stock.

2. In a wok or large skillet, heat oil over medium heat. Add garlic and onion and cook until soft but not browned. Add shrimp and pork and stir-fry just until shrimp begin to turn pink. Add reserved stock, bring to a boil, and simmer 5 minutes. Season to taste with soy sauce and pepper.

3. Add rice sticks to wok and cook, stirring, until noodles have absorbed all but ¼ cup of the stock. Add vegetables; cook until mixture is nearly dry. Transfer to serving plate and garnish with eggs and coriander. Pass additional fish sauce at table.

Serves 4 as a main dish, 6 to 8 with other dishes.

FRESH RICE NOODLES

For those who do not have easy access to an Asian market, here is a recipe for fresh rice sheets and noodles adapted from *Asian Pasta* by Linda Burum (Aris, 1985).

- 1 cup rice flour
- 5 tablespoons tapioca starch (see Note)
- 4 tablespoons wheat starch (see Note)
- 1 teaspoon kosher salt
- 2 cups plus 2 tablespoons water
- 5 teaspoons oil, plus oil to grease pans

1. Combine rice flour, tapioca starch, wheat starch, salt, and water and stir until smooth. Strain batter through a fine strainer and stir in 5 teaspoons oil. Let batter rest 30 minutes.

2. Lightly oil a baking sheet and two 8- by 8-inch or 9- by 9-inch square cake pans. Place a steaming rack in a wok and add water to just below rack. Bring to a boil and have additional boiling water ready to replenish steamer.

3. Stir batter very well and pour enough into one of the cake pans to cover bottom, about ½ cup. Set pan on steaming rack, cover wok, and steam 5 minutes. Remove lid, being careful not to let condensed water drip on rice sheet. Remove cake pan; cool in a sink or larger pan filled with ½ inch cold water. Meanwhile, fill and steam the other cake pan.

4. Loosen the cooled rice sheet from the first pan and roll it out onto the oiled baking sheet. Turn over rice sheet to lightly oil both sides, then transfer to a platter. Repeat cooking, cooling, and oiling steps with remaining batter.

5. Stack rice sheets on a plate, cover with plastic wrap, and refrigerate at least 2 hours before cutting into noodles or adding stuffings.

Makes eight 8-inch-square sheets, about 2 pounds.

Note Tapioca starch and wheat starch are both pure white, silky textured powders, available in 1-pound bags in well-stocked Asian markets.

STIR-FRIED TWO NOODLES
Hokkien mee
Singapore

This is a favorite street snack among the Chinese in many Southeast Asian cities. *Hokkien* is the local pronunciation of *Fujian* (*Fukien*) province in southeast China, the origin of many Chinese emigrants over the years. In a typical noodle-vendor's stand, the pork and shellfish are cooked in a stock that simmers for hours, picking up more flavor all the time. In this home version, the extra flavor comes from reducing the stock after cooking the meats.

> 1 cup each *water and Basic Chicken Stock (see page 62)*
> 1 tablespoon *light or dark soy sauce*
> ½ pound *pork shoulder, in one piece*
> ¼ pound *squid, cleaned and cut up (see page 55)*
> ¼ pound *raw shrimp in the shell*
> 2 tablespoons *oil or lard*
> 3 unpeeled *cloves garlic, crushed*
> 6 ounces *thin egg noodles, boiled, drained, and tossed in a little oil*
> 4 ounces *thick rice sticks (see Note), soaked and drained*
> 2 cups *bean sprouts*
> ¼ cup *Chinese chives or garlic chives, cut into 1-inch lengths*

1. In a small saucepan combine water, stock, soy sauce, and pork. Bring to a boil, reduce heat, and simmer until meat is tender. Remove meat and set aside. Return stock to a boil. Add squid and cook 30 seconds. Remove and set aside. Cook shrimp 2 to 3 minutes. Drain and set aside, reserving stock. Peel shrimp and devein if necessary. (For additional flavor, add shrimp shells to stock and simmer 10 minutes longer.)

2. Bring stock to a boil and reduce by half. Strain stock. (The recipe may be prepared to this point several hours ahead.)

3. Slice pork into bite-sized pieces. In a wok or large skillet, heat oil or lard and garlic to near smoking. Remove and discard garlic cloves when they brown. Add noodles and rice sticks and stir-fry until they are lightly browned in places. Add stock, cover, and cook 2 minutes. Remove cover, add pork, squid, shrimp, and bean sprouts, and continue stirring and cooking until noodles have absorbed most of the liquid, about two minutes. Transfer to serving platter and garnish with Chinese chives.

Serves 4 with other dishes.

<u>Note</u> The authentic rice noodle for this dish is a thicker rice stick called *lai fen* in China and *pancit luglug* in the Philippines, but ordinary thin rice sticks may be used.

MEE KROB
Crisp-fried noodles
Thailand

This special-occasion noodle dish is a favorite in many Thai restaurants. Some versions are extremely sweet and sticky; this version is less so, but the important flavors are still sweet, sour, and salty in that order. Be sure to use a large enough pan for saucing the noodles (step 5); a 14-inch wok is ideal.

> 2 tablespoons each *fish sauce and dark soy sauce*
> *Juice of 2 limes*
> 3 tablespoons *vinegar*
> ¼ cup *brown sugar or half brown and half palm sugar*
> *Oil, for deep-frying*
> 6 ounces *rice sticks*
> 4 eggs, *lightly beaten*
> 1 medium *onion, finely diced*
> 3 cloves *garlic, minced*
> 1 small *red or green chile, seeds removed, finely minced*
> ¾ pound *minced pork, diced chicken, or peeled shrimp, or a mixture*
> 1 or 2 *green onions, sliced, for garnish*

1. In a small bowl, combine fish sauce, soy sauce, lime juice, vinegar, and sugar and set aside.

2. In a wok or deep skillet, heat oil to 350° F. Drop approximately an ounce of rice sticks into the oil; they will puff up and rise to the top of the oil in only a few seconds. Turn them over once and fry until crisp, about 15 seconds in all. Transfer finished noodles to a pan lined with paper towels and continue frying the batter in small batches. Keep noodles warm in a low oven.

3. Dip a hand in the beaten egg and, holding your hand approximately 8 inches above the hot oil, drizzle egg over the surface in a random pattern. Continue with about half the egg mixture, forming a lacy network of egg. Fry until golden brown on underside, turn over once, and brown other side. Transfer to a plate and drain on paper towels. Repeat with remaining egg.

4. Heat a second wok over medium-high heat and add approximately 2 tablespoons oil from the first wok. Add onion, garlic, and chile and cook until they are fragrant. Add meats or shrimp and stir-fry just until done.

5. Stir sugar mixture and add to wok. Bring to a boil and cook until slightly thickened. Reduce heat to low and add about a quarter of the fried noodles and eggs. Stir together and toss to break up noodle clumps and coat with sauce. Continue adding noodles and eggs in batches until all are coated with sauce. Transfer to serving platter and garnish with sliced green onion.

Serves 4 with other dishes.

Perhaps the most famous and popular Thai noodle dish is Mee Krob, a jumble of crisp fried rice noodles tossed in a sweet-and-sour sauce.

THAI CUISINE

No cuisine of Southeast Asia has captured the interest of Americans more than that of Thailand, and for good reason. Thai food combines all the exuberant tropical flavors of Southeast Asia, but is governed by a sense of balance and contrast—of flavors, colors, textures—which rivals that of Chinese cuisine. Much authentic Thai food is quite hot, but the chiles always work in harmony with other ingredients, rather than dominating the dish.

The Thai cuisine that has become popular in the West comes mainly from the southern part of the country and is derived from the cuisine of the royal court. Rich, fragrant curries of meats, poultry, and shellfish are based on carefully blended seasoning pastes, fresh herbs, and coconut milk. Seafood, especially shellfish, is abundant in the south. Elaborately carved fruits and vegetables are another feature of the royal culinary style. Southern Thai dishes often include some sugar to balance the other flavors, but few are really sweet; an exception is the fried noodle dish Mee Krob (see page 110).

Farther north the diet is somewhat simpler; northern Thais, like the closely related Laotians, prefer glutinous rice to long grain and use more freshwater fish than seafood. Raw Beef Salad With Roasted Vegetables (see page 94), a dish of highly seasoned minced raw meat, is typical of both northern Thailand and Laos.

PAD THAI
Stir-fried rice noodles
Thailand

This variable Thai dish is popular for lunch. Most versions use some tomato, as much for color as for flavor. You can substitute other meats or shellfish and make the sauce more or less hot. For a vegetarian version, omit the meats and substitute pieces of Fried Tofu (see page 44).

- ½ *pound flat rice noodles (chantaboon)*
- 1 *teaspoon vinegar*
- 3 *tablespoons fish sauce*
- 1 *teaspoon sugar*
- 1 *tablespoon tomato paste*
- 3 *to 4 tablespoons oil*
- 1 *tablespoon minced garlic*
- ½ *teaspoon sambal ulek or ground dried chile*
- ¼ *pound small raw shrimp, peeled and deveined*
- ¼ *pound minced pork or chicken*
- 2 *eggs, lightly beaten*
- 1 *cup bean sprouts*

Garnishes

- 1 *tablespoon dried shrimp, ground in a mortar or finely minced*
- 2 *tablespoons peanuts, toasted and chopped*
- 1 *fresh red chile, sliced*
- 1 *green onion, thinly sliced*

1. In a bowl soak noodles in warm water until soft, about 15 minutes. In another bowl combine vinegar, fish sauce, sugar, and tomato paste; stir to dissolve sugar. Set mixture aside. Drain noodles and set aside in colander.

2. In a wok or deep skillet, heat 3 tablespoons oil over medium-high heat until a bit of garlic sizzles. Add garlic and sambal ulek and stir-fry until fragrant. Add shrimp and pork and stir-fry until they lose their raw color. Add tomato paste mixture and bring to a boil. Toss noodles in sauce and cook, stirring, until noodles have absorbed sauce.

3. Use a spatula to lift or push the noodle mass away from the center of the pan. If pan looks dry, add another tablespoon of oil. Add eggs,

allow to cook 10 to 15 seconds, then set noodle mass on top of egg. Stir and fold eggs and noodles together until egg is set. Stir in bean sprouts.

4. Serve with garnishes sprinkled on in this order: first dried shrimp, then peanuts, chile, and green onion.

Serves 3 to 4 as a main dish, 6 or more with other dishes.

RICE NOODLES WITH BROCCOLI
Rad na gwaytio
Thailand

If possible use fresh rice noodles for this dish. If you make them as directed on page 109, cut them into ⅜-inch-wide strips. As a last resort use cooked and drained flat rice noodles (*chantaboon*).

- 12 *ounces fresh rice noodles*
- 4 *teaspoons oyster sauce (available in Asian markets)*
- 1 *tablespoon each fish sauce and water*
- ½ *teaspoon cornstarch*
- 2 *to 3 tablespoons oil*
- 1 *tablespoon minced garlic*
- ½ *pound boneless pork or chicken breast, in thin strips*
- 2 *teaspoons dark soy sauce*
- 2 *cups sliced and blanched broccoli or Chinese broccoli*
- ¾ *cup Basic Chicken Stock (see page 62)*

1. In a colander pour hot water over noodles to soften them slightly and pull apart; separate. Set aside; drain.

2. In a small bowl combine oyster sauce, fish sauce, water, and cornstarch and stir to dissolve.

3. Heat wok over medium-high heat and add 2 tablespoons oil. Add garlic and pork or chicken and stir-fry until meat just loses its raw color. Add drained noodles and stir-fry until slightly browned in places. Stir in dark soy sauce and toss to color noodles evenly, then add broccoli, oyster-sauce mixture, and stock. Cook, stirring and scraping pan, until sauce is thick and reduced by one half. Transfer to serving bowl or platter and arrange broccoli on top.

Serves 3 to 4 as a main dish.

SALADS

Western labels do not necessarily describe Asian eating patterns. The cuisines of Southeast Asia include many dishes of meats, vegetables, fruits, seeds, or a combination of these served cold or at room temperature. We tend to call these dishes salads even though they are served with the rest of the meal rather than as a separate course.

The following recipes give an idea of the range of Southeast Asian salads. Some are substantial enough to serve as main dishes for lunch, but most are intended to accompany other dishes. Note the sparing use of oil compared to Western salads, an example of the healthful qualities of Southeast Asian cooking.

GINGER SALAD
Burma

Crunchy sesame seeds, piquant ginger, and garlic-infused oil flavor this unusual salad.

> 3 tablespoons oil
> 2 tablespoons minced garlic
> ¼ cup yellow split peas
> ¼ cup dried fava beans
>   Oil, for deep-frying
> ⅓ cup peanuts
> 1 tablespoon lime or lemon juice
> 1 teaspoon fish sauce
>   Pinch salt
> ½ cup shredded cabbage
> 2 tablespoons sesame seeds, toasted in a dry skillet
> ¼ cup coconut flakes or shreds, toasted in a dry skillet
> 2 tablespoons each shredded ginger and minced yellow onion
> 1 fresh red or green chile, thinly sliced, seeds removed from slices
> 2 tablespoons dried shrimp, finely chopped or ground in a mortar
>   Lemon or lime wedges, to taste

1. In a small skillet heat 3 tablespoons oil over very low heat. Add garlic and cook gently until lightly browned. Do not let garlic cook too quickly or too dark or it will become bitter. Strain oil through a fine sieve into a bowl. Spread garlic on a paper towel to drain.

2. Boil split peas until just barely cooked; drain. Boil favas until skins soften, remove from water, peel off skins, and return beans to water to cook until they swell and begin to split. Drain.

3. In a wok or saucepan, heat oil to 350° F. Fry peanuts until lightly browned; drain. Fry favas until crisp and golden brown; drain. Fry split peas until crisp; drain. (A fine wire sieve dipped in the frying oil is an easy way to contain these ingredients.)

4. In a small bowl combine lime juice, fish sauce, and salt; stir to dissolve. Place cabbage in center of a large shallow bowl or plate and arrange fried and toasted ingredients, ginger, onion, and chile in small piles around outside. Sprinkle dried shrimp and fried garlic on top. To serve, pour cooled garlic oil and lime juice mixture over all and toss at table with spoon and fork to combine. Serve with lemon wedges to season each serving to taste.

Serves 4 with other dishes.

CUCUMBER SALAD

The cool, mild flavor and crisp texture of cucumber make it especially good with highly seasoned dishes. Most versions contain chile, sugar, vinegar or lime juice, and something salty, varied to taste.

> 2 tablespoons lime juice or rice vinegar
> 1 tablespoon water
> 1 teaspoon sugar
> ¼ teaspoon kosher salt
> 2 cups sliced cucumber
> ¼ cup thinly sliced onion
> 1 fresh red or green chile, thinly sliced, loose seeds removed
>   Lettuce leaves
> 1 tablespoon dried shrimp, pounded or ground (optional)
>   Fresh coriander or mint leaves (optional)

In a medium bowl, combine lime juice, water, sugar, and salt and stir to dissolve. Add cucumber, onion, and chile and toss to dress. Serve on a plate lined with lettuce leaves, garnished if desired with ground shrimp and coriander or mint leaves.

Serves 4 to 6 with other dishes.

CHICKEN AND GREEN PAPAYA SALAD
Cambodia

Variations on this theme—cooked meats served cold with shredded vegetables and a spicy lime-and-fish-sauce dressing—are found throughout Southeast Asia. This Cambodian version uses green (unripe) papaya as a vegetable.

> 1 teaspoon chopped garlic
> 1 tablespoon oil
> 1 cup shredded green papaya
> 1 medium carrot, shredded
> 12 mint leaves
> 1 cooked chicken breast, skinned, boned, and shredded by hand
> ¼ cup toasted peanuts, chopped
> 1 green onion, finely sliced
> ⅓ cup Spicy Lime Sauce (see page 35)

Sauté garlic in oil over medium heat until lightly browned and allow to cool slightly. Combine papaya, carrot, mint, chicken, peanuts, and green onion in a salad bowl. Add garlic and oil and lime sauce. Toss by hand, squeezing mixture lightly to combine flavors more thoroughly. Serve on a lettuce leaf.

Serves 4 as an appetizer.

Pork Skin Salad Reserve a 6-inch square of skin from a pork shoulder or fresh leg. Cut away as much fat as possible from the inside and poach skin in water or stock until quite tender, about 30 minutes. Cut away any more fat that may be clinging to inside and cut into fine julienne. Use in place of chicken in above recipe; let mixture stand 30 minutes before serving.

An assortment of crunchy seeds, fiery chiles, raw onion, and a most unusual vegetable—tea leaves—await final tossing to make Burmese Green Tea Salad.

GREEN TEA SALAD
Lap pat dok
Burma

This salad is similar to Ginger Salad, but with one striking addition: green tea leaves used as a vegetable. The authentic version uses fresh tea leaves that have been stored in fresh water (preferably running water) for several months before being used. Since these leaves are virtually unobtainable here, we have to make do with dried tea. Use a large-leafed variety such as the Chinese Pouchong or Dragon Well.

> ¼ cup loose-pack green tea
> 2 to 3 tablespoons oil
> 2 tablespoons sliced garlic
> ¼ cup yellow split peas
> ¼ cup peanuts
>   Oil, for deep-frying
> 1½ tablespoons lime or
>   lemon juice
> 2 teaspoons fish sauce
>   Pinch salt
> ¼ cup sesame seeds, toasted in
>   a dry skillet
> 2 tablespoons minced yellow
>   onion
> 1 fresh red or green chile,
>   thinly sliced, seeds removed
>   from slices
>   Lemon or lime wedges, to taste

1. One to two days ahead: Place tea leaves in a bowl or teapot and cover with 2 cups boiling water. Let steep 5 minutes and strain. Return leaves to bowl and cover with cold water. Let steep overnight, drain, and cover again with cold water. Continue changing water every hour or so until water no longer stains green. Store leaves in water in refrigerator until ready to use.

2. In a small skillet heat 2 to 3 tablespoons oil over very low heat. Add garlic and cook gently until lightly browned. Do not let garlic cook too quickly or too dark or it will become bitter. Strain oil through a fine sieve into a bowl. Spread garlic on a paper towel to drain.

3. When oil has cooled, drain tea leaves thoroughly and moisten with 1 tablespoon garlic oil. Set aside.

4. Boil split peas until just barely cooked; drain. In a wok or saucepan, heat oil to 350° F. Fry split peas until crisp; drain. Fry peanuts in same oil until lightly browned; drain. (A fine wire sieve dipped in the frying oil is an easy way to contain these ingredients.)

5. In a small bowl, combine lime juice, fish sauce, and salt; stir to dissolve. Place tea leaves in center of a large shallow bowl or plate and arrange fried and toasted ingredients, onion, and chile in small piles around outside. Salad may be assembled up to an hour ahead of serving. To serve, pour lime juice mixture over all at table and toss with spoon and fork to combine. Season each serving to taste with lemon or lime wedges.

Serves 4 with other dishes.

COCONUT SHRIMP SALAD
Thailand

In this salad, a relative of the Latin American ceviche and the Polynesian *poisson cru*, the shrimp is "cooked" by marinating it in lime juice. A very brief cure is authentic, but if you prefer, marinate the shrimp longer (up to 12 hours) for more complete cooking.

> ½ pound small shrimp (40 or
>   more per pound), peeled and
>   deveined
> ¼ cup lime or lemon juice
> ½ cup medium coconut milk (see
>   page 38)
> 1 shallot, halved and sliced
>   Salt, to taste
> 1 or 2 small red or green chiles,
>   sliced crosswise

1. Rinse shrimp and drain. Place in a small bowl, toss with lime juice, and marinate 10 to 15 minutes, stirring occasionally. Shrimp should just begin to get firm and opaque. Drain.

2. Combine shrimp, coconut milk, and shallot and chill until ready to serve. Salt to taste. Arrange shrimp on a plate, scatter with chiles, and spoon dressing over all.

Serves 4 with other dishes.

COCONUT AND VEGETABLE SALAD
Urap
Indonesia

According to some authorities, this ceremonial dish can be made with either raw or cooked vegetables, but never both together. Whether or not you mix them, try to get fresh coconut, as this dish relies heavily on the flavor and texture of grated coconut. If only dried is available, refresh it by soaking briefly in cool water.

> ½ teaspoon dried shrimp paste
> 1 shallot
> 1 clove garlic
> 1 tablespoon minced fresh
>   galangal or krachai
>   (optional, but do not substi-
>   tute ground)
> ½ teaspoon minced fresh chile
>   or sambal ulek
>   Tamarind Water (see page
>   34), made with 1 teaspoon
>   tamarind and 1 tablespoon
>   water
>   Pinch sugar
> 1 cup assorted vegetables (a
>   variety of the following):
>   shredded spinach or cabbage,
>   bean sprouts, sliced green
>   beans or snow peas, shredded
>   bamboo shoots, sliced or
>   julienned zucchini or chayote
> ½ cup grated coconut
>   Watercress or fresh coriander,
>   for garnish

1. Wrap shrimp paste in a square of aluminum foil and toast 2 to 3 minutes in a skillet or over a charcoal fire; cool. Unwrap and place in a mortar with shallot, garlic, galangal (if used), and chile; pound to a paste. Blend in Tamarind Water and sugar.

2. Blanch or steam vegetables separately until almost done; allow to cool; combine. Mix coconut and dressing and add to vegetables; toss until mixed. Garnish with watercress.

Serves 4 with other dishes.

Variation If you prefer a salad of all raw vegetables, try cucumbers, radishes, sliced or grated carrots, bean sprouts, lettuce, watercress, and fresh herbs such as mint and basil.

MIXED VEGETABLE SALAD WITH PEANUT SAUCE
Gado-gado
Indonesia

This is a rather free-form salad of lightly cooked vegetables; the exact contents depend on what is available. What makes it *gado-gado* is the dressing, a creamy peanut sauce.

    1 package firm (Chinese-style)
        tofu
    1 teaspoon kecap manis
        Oil, for deep-frying
    6 cups vegetables (a variety of
        the following): cabbage, in
        1-inch squares; bean sprouts;
        carrots, sliced or julienned;
        green beans, in 2-inch pieces;
        potatoes or sweet potatoes, in
        large dice; sliced cucumbers;
        watercress sprigs; tomato
        wedges
        Hard-cooked eggs, for garnish
        Fried Onion Flakes (see
        page 35), for garnish

Gado-Gado Sauce

    1 tablespoon minced garlic
    2 tablespoons minced shallot
    1 tablespoon minced fresh
        galangal or 1 teaspoon
        ground
    1 teaspoon dried shrimp paste
    ½ teaspoon ground dried chile
        or ¼ teaspoon sambal ulek
    1 cup oil
    ½ cup raw peanuts
    1 teaspoon brown or palm
        sugar
    1 cup thin coconut milk
        (see page 38)
        Salt, to taste
        Juice of ½ lime, to taste

1. Remove tofu from package and drain. Place on a plate lined with cloth or paper towels, top with another layer of towel and an inverted plate, and place a weight of a pound or more on top. Let stand 30 minutes, unwrap, and discard liquid. Cut tofu into bite-sized squares or triangles and sprinkle with kecap manis. Fry in 350° F oil until golden brown and puffy; transfer to paper towels to drain. Reserve oil to cook peanuts.

2. One at a time, blanch vegetables in lightly salted water, rinsing them in cold water to stop cooking as soon as they reach the desired degree of doneness. Cabbage and bean sprouts require only a few seconds; carrots, green beans, and potatoes may take several minutes depending on size and tenderness. Do not blanch cucumbers, watercress, and tomatoes; use them raw.

3. Place Gado-Gado Sauce in a small bowl in the center of a large platter. Arrange vegetables on platter around sauce. Garnish with wedges or slices of hard-cooked egg and fried onion flakes. To serve, spoon some sauce onto each plate and dip vegetables into sauce.

Serves 4 to 6 with other dishes.

Gado-Gado Sauce

1. *To prepare sauce in a mortar:* Pound garlic, shallot, galangal, shrimp paste, and chile to a paste. *To prepare sauce in a blender:* Chop together in a 1-cup jar.

2. In a wok or deep skillet, heat oil over medium-high heat until a peanut sizzles on contact. Fry peanuts until lightly browned; transfer to paper towels to drain. When peanuts have cooled, grind in a mortar or food processor to a coarse, grainy paste, adding a little oil if necessary to facilitate blending. (May be made up to a week ahead and stored covered in refrigerator.)

3. Remove all but 2 tablespoons oil from pan and reserve for another use. Return pan to medium-low heat and add pounded mixture. Cook until quite fragrant, but do not burn. Add peanuts, sugar, and coconut milk and bring to a boil, stirring. Simmer until thick and season to taste with salt and lime juice. Allow to cool to room temperature before serving.

Makes 1 cup.

FRUIT AND SHRIMP SALAD
Yam Polamai
Thailand

This unusual recipe comes from Chalie Amatyakul, director of the Thai Cooking School at the Oriental, in Bangkok. There it is made with such local fruits as mangosteen, roseapple, and pomelo. A kind of oversized grapefruit, pomelo is often available around the Asian New Year, in January or February. Exotic fruits are showing up in our markets all the time, so feel free to improvise.

    2 cups assorted fruits (a variety
        of the following): sliced green
        apples; pears; tangerine
        sections; grapefruit or pomelo;
        grapes; strawberries; firm
        papaya; oranges
    2 tablespoons oil
    1 shallot, thinly sliced
    3 cloves garlic, thinly sliced
        Juice of 1 lime
    1 teaspoon kosher salt
    1 teaspoon sugar, or to taste
        (optional)
    ¼ cup cooked shrimp
    2 tablespoons chopped toasted
        peanuts
    1 fresh red chile, seeded and
        finely shredded

1. Cut fruit into bite-sized pieces. If using pomelo, peel individual sections and break apart into grains about the size of a grape seed. If grapes contain seeds, split and seed them. Toss apple or pear slices in a little citrus juice to keep them from oxidizing.

2. In a small skillet or saucepan, heat oil over low heat and gently fry shallot and garlic until lightly browned. Remove and drain on paper towels.

3. In a medium bowl, combine lime juice, salt, and sugar (if used) and stir to dissolve. Add fruits, shrimp, and half the garlic and shallot and toss to coat evenly with dressing. Taste and adjust seasoning if necessary. Transfer to serving dish and garnish with remaining garlic and shallot, peanuts, and chile.

Serves 4 with other dishes.

Variation Use cooked and shredded chicken or pork in place of shrimp.

A startling combination of sweet and tart fruits, shrimp, peanuts, chiles, shallots, and garlic adds up to a surprisingly delicious Thai salad.

Crisp fried Lumpia Shanghai, the Philippine version of egg rolls, are delicious dipped in either a sweet-and-sour sauce or a mixture of vinegar, garlic, and fish sauce.

WRAPPED FOODS: SPRING ROLLS AND LUMPIA

This is a loose category of foods rolled in edible wrappers, and best eaten with fingers. Some, like the Vietnamese spring rolls and the Philippine *lumpia,* are deep-fried in a noodle- or pancakelike wrapper. Others are eaten fresh—that is, without additional cooking.

Rice Papers In Vietnam and Cambodia, rice papers (*banh trang*) are used both for the fried crab rolls known as *cha gio* and as a fresh wrapper for cooked meats. These translucent rounds are made of rice starch and water and dried on woven bamboo mats, which leave crosshatch markings. Most now come from Thailand, in packages labeled in Vietnamese. Rice papers must be moistened to make them flexible enough to roll. This may be done with a pastry brush, by misting with a spray bottle, or even by dipping the sheets in water. But the easiest way is to stack them between kitchen towels for about 5 minutes (see page 121).

Lumpia Wrappers There are two types of lumpia wrappers. One is round, made of flour and water; a recipe appears on page 119. The other type is square and has a consistency of a very thin egg noodle. These are often labeled egg roll skins, but they are much thinner than Chinese egg roll wrappers. The round kind can be used for either fresh or fried lumpia, but the square ones are only suitable for frying. Both types are sold fresh and frozen. Tightly wrapped, they will keep a week or more in the refrigerator after thawing.

Lettuce Edible leaves are also popular wrappers in Southeast Asia. Lettuce-Wrapped Meatballs (see page 121) is a typical example. Lettuce can serve as a second wrap for Meatballs Wrapped in Noodles (see page 47).

Lumpia Sauces A highly seasoned sauce invariably accompanies lumpia. Both Sweet-and-Sour Sauce (see 119) and Sweet Lumpia Sauce (see page 120) may be used interchangeably for fresh or fried lumpia. Another dipping sauce for fried lumpia mixes soy sauce or fish sauce, vinegar, and chopped garlic to taste.

FRIED EGG ROLLS
Lumpia shanghai
Philippines

The Philippines produce several versions of the ubiquitous spring roll. This one gets its name from its Chinese-style filling; another possibility is to use the filling for Fresh Lumpia (see page 120), but cut the meats and vegetables into smaller pieces and omit lettuce leaves. There are also sweet fried lumpia, filled with sweet potatoes or bananas, jackfruit, or other fruits.

> ½ pound finely ground pork or beef
> ¼ cup minced green onion
> 1 tablespoon each minced ginger and garlic
> 4 black mushroom caps, soaked, drained, and finely diced
> ¼ cup finely diced water chestnuts or jicama
> 1 tablespoon fish sauce
> 1 egg
> Freshly ground pepper, to taste
> 16 lumpia wrappers (the type labeled egg-roll skins, or homemade, see below)
> Oil, for deep frying

Sweet-and-Sour Sauce

> ½ cup water or Basic Chicken Stock (see page 62)
> 2 tablespoons soy sauce
> 3 tablespoons rice vinegar or cider vinegar
> 2 tablespoons brown sugar
> 2 tablespoons ketchup
> Dash liquid hot-pepper sauce
> 1 teaspoon cornstarch dissolved in 1 tablespoon water

1. In a bowl, combine pork, green onion, ginger, garlic, mushrooms, water chestnuts, and fish sauce and blend thoroughly. Beat egg lightly and add to pork mixture, reserving a teaspoon or so for sealing rolls. Season generously with pepper. Sauté a small piece of filling, taste and adjust seasoning.

2. Spread about 2 tablespoons filling diagonally across the middle of a wrapper. Roll and seal as shown in Preparing Spring Rolls and Lumpia, page 121. Lumpia may be rolled up to 1 hour ahead of frying.

3. Heat oil in fryer to 350° F. Fry lumpia a few at a time until golden brown; drain on paper towels. Serve immediately or keep warm in oven. Serve with Sweet-and-Sour Sauce or Sweet Lumpia Sauce (see page 120).

Serves 8 as an appetizer.

Sweet-and-Sour Sauce In a saucepan combine water, soy sauce, vinegar, sugar, ketchup, and hot-pepper sauce and bring to a boil. Season to taste and simmer 5 minutes. Stir in dissolved cornstarch; cook until lightly thickened and glossy.

Makes ⅔ cup.

LUMPIA WRAPPERS I
Philippines

Here are two versions of homemade *lumpia* wrappers. The first is made with egg, the second without. Both Lumpia Wrappers I and Lumpia Wrappers II can be used interchangeably for fresh or fried lumpia.

> 1 egg
> ½ cup plus 2 tablespoons water
> ⅔ cup cornstarch
> Pinch salt

Combine ingredients and stir until smooth; let stand 15 minutes. Lightly oil an 8-inch nonstick skillet or crêpe pan over medium heat. Pour a scant 2 tablespoons batter into pan and quickly tilt and swirl to cover bottom with batter. Cook until edges begin to peel away from pan, about 1 minute. Lift edge with fingertips or spatula, turn, cook 30 seconds on second side, and turn out onto a plate. Continue with remaining batter.

Makes 8 wrappers.

LUMPIA WRAPPERS II

> 1¼ cups water
> 1 cup cake flour, sifted
> Pinch salt

Combine ingredients and stir until smooth; let stand 15 minutes. Batter should have the consistency of thick cream. Preheat and oil pan as above, but instead of pouring batter into pan, brush it on with a wide pastry brush, adding a second or third coat as necessary to fill in gaps and thin spots. This makes an especially delicate wrapper.

Makes 8 wrappers.

CRAB OR SHRIMP ROLLS
Cha gio
Vietnam

Rice papers make a very crisp, almost transparent wrapper for these delightful bites. Try them wrapped in a lettuce leaf, with a mint leaf tucked in, and dipped in Nuoc Mam Sauce.

> 1½ ounces bean threads
> ⅓ pound finely ground uncooked pork
> ¼ pound cooked crabmeat or minced cooked shrimp
> 1 tablespoon cloud ears, soaked, drained, and finely shredded
> ½ cup minced green or yellow onion
> 1 clove garlic, minced
> Pinch freshly ground pepper
> 6 eight-inch round rice papers, moistened
> 1 egg, beaten
> Oil, for deep-frying
> Nuoc Mam Sauce (see page 35); for accompaniment

1. Soak bean threads in water until soft. Drain and cut into 1-inch lengths. Combine with pork, crab or shrimp, cloud ears, onion, garlic, and pepper and blend thoroughly.

2. Moisten rice papers as shown in Preparing Spring Rolls and Lumpia, step 1, page 121. Cut a sheet into quarters, keeping remainder covered with damp towels. Fill each roll with about 1 tablespoon filling, roll up, and seal with beaten egg, as shown in steps 2 through 4. Rolls may be prepared to this point 1 to 2 hours before frying; cover with damp towel to prevent drying.

3. Fry rolls a few at a time in 375° F oil until crisp and golden brown. Test a roll to be sure filling is cooked; if not, lower heat to 350° F and fry a little longer. Drain on paper towels and serve immediately, or keep warm. Serve with Nuoc Mam Sauce.

Serves 6 to 8 as an appetizer.

Some foods just seem to taste better when eaten without cutlery. Tender lettuce leaves make an ideal package for these Cambodian meatballs and their various garnishes.

FRESH LUMPIA
Philippines

In this version of *lumpia*, the cooked filling is first wrapped in a lettuce leaf, then rolled in the lumpia wrapper and eaten without any further cooking. Fresh homemade wrappers are best for this purpose.

> 16 lettuce leaves (butter, red leaf, or heart leaves of romaine)
> 16 Lumpia Wrappers (see page 119)
>   Sweet Lumpia Sauce or Sweet-and-Sour Sauce (see page 119)
> 1   tablespoon oil
> 1   Chinese sausage, thinly sliced, or 3 thick slices bacon, diced and blanched
> 2   tablespoons garlic
> 1   cup finely diced boiling potatoes
> 1   small onion, diced
> ½   cup shredded bamboo shoots or hearts of palm
> ¼   cup shredded cabbage
> ½   pound cooked pork or chicken, diced (see Note)
> ¼   pound cooked shrimp, diced
>   Salt and freshly ground pepper, to taste

Sweet Lumpia Sauce

> 1   cup chicken or meat broth
> ⅓   cup brown sugar
> 4   cloves garlic, crushed
> 1½ teaspoons cornstarch dissolved in 2 tablespoons soy sauce
>   Liquid hot-pepper sauce, to taste (optional)

1. Have lettuce leaves and wrappers ready on a platter, with sauce in a bowl alongside.

2. In a wok or skillet, heat oil over medium-low heat and cook sausage or bacon until lightly browned. Add garlic and cook until fragrant. Add potatoes and onion and cook until potatoes are tender. Add bamboo shoots or hearts of palm, cabbage, pork or chicken, and shrimp and stir-fry together until mixture is heated through. Season to taste with salt and pepper and transfer to a serving bowl.

3. To serve, spoon filling into the center of a lettuce leaf, add sauce to taste, then roll the leaf inside a wrapper, enclosing the filling and the base of the leaf.

Serves 4 to 6 as an appetizer.

Sweet Lumpia Sauce In a small saucepan combine broth, sugar, and garlic and bring to a boil, stirring to dissolve sugar. Reduce mixture by one third, stir in dissolved cornstarch, and cook until thickened and glossy. Add a few drops of hot-pepper sauce, if desired.

Makes ¾ cup.

<u>Note</u> If you cook pork or chicken especially for the lumpia, reserve the broth for the Sweet Lumpia Sauce; otherwise use Basic Chicken Stock (see page 62).

LETTUCE-WRAPPED MEATBALLS
Apsara trong kroeung
Cambodia

Meatballs are fun to eat with fingers. Here, a lettuce leaf keeps the sauce off your fingers and holds tasty nuggets of ginger, garlic, and lime.

> *Oil, for deep-frying*
> ½ *ounce bean threads*
> ½ *pound finely minced or ground pork or beef*
> 1 *teaspoon fish sauce*
> ½ *cup Basic Chicken Stock (see page 62)*
> *Peanut Sauce I or II (see page 36)*
> *Tender lettuce leaves (butter, limestone, or Boston)*
> 1 *tablespoon finely diced ginger (⅛-inch cubes)*
> 1 *lime, cut with peel into fine dice*
> 2 *tablespoons minced pickled garlic (see Note)*

1. In a wok or deep skillet, heat oil at least 1 inch deep to 350° F. Break apart bundle of bean threads and drop into oil. They will puff and rise almost instantly. Turn after 10 seconds or so and fry on the other side another 10 seconds. Remove; drain. When cool enough to handle, break into pieces 1 inch or less in length.

2. Remove all but 1 tablespoon oil from pan. Mix pork and fish sauce; form into 1-inch balls. Return pan to medium heat and lightly brown meatballs. Add stock, cover, and simmer until meatballs are done.

3. Place peanut sauce in a small bowl. Cut meatballs almost into quarters, leaving the wedges attached at the base. Arrange a tray or platter with meatballs, lettuce leaves, bean threads, ginger, lime, and garlic in separate piles or small dishes. To serve, place a piece of meatball in a lettuce leaf and spoon in garnishes and sauce.

Serves 4 with other dishes.

<u>Note</u> Pickled garlic is available in Asian groceries; or use fresh blanched garlic instead.

Step-by-Step

PREPARING SPRING ROLLS AND LUMPIA

1. *To soften rice papers before rolling, layer them between damp kitchen towels, and let stand until flexible (about 5 minutes). When soft, cut into quarters.*

2. *Place filling near curved edge of paper, leaving space on both ends to seal ends of roll.*

3. *Roll paper partly around filling, tuck in corners; continue rolling.*

4. *Moisten tip of triangle with beaten egg to seal.*

5. *Start frying rolls sealed side down to ensure a good seal.*

6. *Square or round lumpia wrappers are rolled in the same way to make longer rolls. Use square wrappers whole, or cut in half as shown.*

A PHILIPPINE MERIENDA

*Fresh Lumpia
(see page 120)*

*Braised Rice Noodles
With Pork and Shrimp
(see page 109)*

Coconut-Milk Cake

Rice-Flour Squares

Banana Fritters

Tea

One legacy of the Spanish colonial period in the Philippines is the sometimes lavish midafternoon merienda. Like English high tea, merienda is practically a meal in itself, combining sweet and savory snacks. This version includes fresh lumpia, a dish of stir-fried noodles, and several Philippine sweets, including an unusual Coconut-Milk Cake topped with grated cheese.

COCONUT-MILK CAKE
Bibingka especial

> 2 *cups flour*
> 1 *teaspoon kosher salt*
> 4 *teaspoons baking powder*
> 3 *eggs, at room temperature*
> ¾ *cup sugar*
> 1¼ *cups thick coconut milk
>   (see page 38)*
> ⅓ *cup grated Parmesan or
>   similar cheese*
> 3 *tablespoons melted butter*

1. Preheat oven to 375° F. Sift flour, salt, and baking powder together and set aside.

2. In a large bowl or electric mixer, beat eggs and sugar together until doubled in volume. Gradually add coconut milk, beating on low speed. Sprinkle flour mixture over top and beat in gently; beat only long enough to incorporate flour. Pour batter into a buttered and floured 9-inch square cake pan.

3. Bake 15 minutes, sprinkle with cheese; continue baking until center of cake springs back when lightly touched, another 15 to 20 minutes. Drizzle with melted butter, allow to cool in pan; cut into squares.

Serves 8 to 10.

RICE-FLOUR SQUARES
Epasol

> 2 *cups glutinous rice flour*
> 2 *cups (14-oz can) thick coconut
>   milk (see page 38)*
> ½ *cup sugar*
> ⅓ *cup grated coconut, toasted*

1. Spread rice flour on a baking sheet and toast in a 375° F oven until lightly browned. Or toast in a dry skillet or wok over medium heat, stirring or shaking pan constantly.

2. In a saucepan, combine coconut milk and sugar and bring to a boil. Reduce heat to low and stir in all but ¼ cup of the toasted flour; mixture will thicken instantly. Remove pan from heat and beat with a wooden spoon until smooth and cool enough to handle. Dust a baking sheet with a little of the remaining toasted flour.

3. Press out dough to a thickness of ¼ inch and chill at least 1 hour. Cut into 2-inch squares or diamonds. Dip pieces in toasted coconut.

Makes 18 to 20 two-inch squares.

BANANA FRITTERS
Maruyang saging

In the Philippines these would be made with the short, thick cooking bananas known as *saba*. Plantains, another cooking variety, will do as a substitute. If neither is available, use ordinary sweet bananas and omit the sugar in the batter.

> 2 *eggs*
> ½ *cup milk*
> 1 *cup flour*
> 1 *teaspoon baking powder*
> 1 *tablespoon sugar*
> ½ *teaspoon kosher salt*
> 4 *ripe saba bananas or 2 ripe
>   plantains or 3 firm but ripe
>   bananas*
>   *Oil, for deep-frying*
>   *Confectioners' sugar
>   (optional)*

1. In a large bowl or electric mixer, combine eggs and milk and beat lightly. Sift flour, baking powder, sugar, and salt together and add to bowl. Combine and beat lightly, just until dry ingredients are incorporated. For best results, let batter rest at least 2 hours and as many as 24 hours, covered and refrigerated, before frying.

2. Peel bananas, split or quarter lengthwise, and cut into 2-inch lengths. Add to batter and toss to coat evenly.

3. Heat oil in wok or frying pan to 375° F. Spoon battered banana pieces into oil a few at a time and fry until golden brown. Drain and serve warm, dusted with Confectioners' sugar if desired.

Makes 16 to 20 fritters.

Sweet Potato Fritters Prepare batter as in above recipe, but substitute 1 cup grated yellow or orange sweet potatoes. Fry by tablespoonfuls.

Makes 24 fritters.

A spread of sweet and savory teatime snacks: Bibingka and Epasol, top; Banana Fritters, left; and filling and wrappers for Fresh Lumpia, at right.

INDEX

127

U.S. MEASURE AND METRIC MEASURE CONVERSION CHART

Formulas for Exact Measures

Rounded Measures for Quick Reference

	Symbol	When you know:	Multiply by:	To find:			
Mass (Weight)	oz	ounces	28.35	grams	1 oz		= 30 g
	lb	pounds	0.45	kilograms	4 oz		= 115 g
	g	grams	0.035	ounces	8 oz		= 225 g
	kg	kilograms	2.2	pounds	16 oz	= 1 lb	= 450 g
					32 oz	= 2 lb	= 900 g
					36 oz	= 2¼ lb	= 1,000 g (1 kg)
Volume	tsp	teaspoons	5.0	milliliters	¼ tsp	= 1/24 oz	= 1 ml
	tbsp	tablespoons	15.0	milliliters	½ tsp	= 1/12 oz	= 2 ml
	fl oz	fluid ounces	29.57	milliliters	1 tsp	= 1/6 oz	= 5 ml
	c	cups	0.24	liters	1 tbsp	= ½ oz	= 15 ml
	pt	pints	0.47	liters	1 c	= 8 oz	= 250 ml
	qt	quarts	0.95	liters	2 c (1 pt)	= 16 oz	= 500 ml
	gal	gallons	3.785	liters	4 c (1 qt)	= 32 oz	= 1 liter
	ml	milliliters	0.034	fluid ounces	4 qt (1 gal)	= 128 oz	= 3¾ liters
Temperature	° F	Fahrenheit	5/9 (after subtracting 32)	Celsius	32° F		= 0° C
	° C	Celsius	9/5 (then add 32)	Fahrenheit	68° F		= 20° C
					212° F		= 100° C